Gina Warren has an amazing heart for ministry and a passion for physical fitness. I believe her passion for seeking the warrior's heart through the holy scriptures, physical fitness, and through fight training with her incredible husband, former professional MMA fighter, Brian "Mr. Unbreakable" Warren, will help others to understand the true meaning of a warrior's heart and duties. As a combat veteran, and former U.S. Army Special Forces Green Beret, I believe this book will help bridge the gap between physical and spiritual warfare. This is a must read!

— ***Don E. Bowen,*** **former U.S. Army Special Forces Green Beret, Judo & BJJ black belt, and member of SAG-AFTRA**

Prophet Gina Guy-Warren is a true Kingdom warrior who has traveled extensively throughout the nations and fought many battles for the Lord. She has discovered the secret to living in victory. This is a must-read book for any serious seekers of God.

— ***Pastor Frank Starks*****, founder, KCWG The Truth, internet radio station**

Prophet Gina Guy-Warren is absolutely, without doubt, the most *authentic* person I know. She always speaks the "Truth N Love" no matter what the cost, and I can assure you that her writing speaks directly from the heart of God. This book will be a life-changing read.

— ***Tami Barthel*****, administrative assistant to the superintendent, Argyle, Texas Independent School District**

I have known Gina Warren for ten years. She has always been on the cutting edge of introducing the movements of God. She has the ability to connect the aspects of spiritual warfare to physical fitness and wellness alongside her powerful husband and ministry partner,

Brian Warren, who excelled as a former MMA fighter and Champion. Gina and Brian are well equipped to compile such a powerful resource to fulfill the sanctification of spirit, soul, and body. This book is literally going to move you into the next dimension of winning in spiritual wellness and warfare.

— ***Apostle Jason Welsh*, lead pastor Amazing Church Lake Elsinore / Church On The R.E.A.L**

I have personally worked with Pastor Gina for the last several years. Her knowledge of homeopathic medicine, natural health remedies, and plant-based solutions to help others heal is truly astonishing. Her natural pathway to health and wellness goes against the norm of prescribing harmful medications. She has the knowledge and a clear vision of how to heal the body using holistic products that are backed by pure science. I look forward to helping her work with tens of thousands in this like-minded pursuit.

— ***Rory Wendell*, 30 Years + private investigation company, owner 35 Fitness World Health, former competitive body builder/semi-pro football player, retired law enforcement**

The Word and the Workout

Prophetic Insight into Physical, Emotional, & Spiritual Fitness

GINA GUY-WARREN

Foreword by
Wendy Alec, Co-Founder, God TV

First Printing

The Way of a Warrior, Book 1 of The Word and the Workout,™ Prophetic Insight into Physical, Emotional, & Spiritual Fitness

Published by Unbreakable Reed, LLC

"A broken reed He will not break, and a dimly burning wick He will not quench; He will bring forth justice in truth." (Isaiah 42:3 AMPCE)

 Some names and identifying details have been changed to protect the privacy of individuals.

Cover design: Kristen Ingebretson

Cover photography: Rude Dog Spice

Interior design: Author Shari McGriff

ISBN: 978-0-578-44086-6

Printed in the United States of America

To my courageous daughters,
Ronni and Lauren.
I'm so proud of the women you've become.
I adore and love you both forever and a day.
—Mommy

CONTENTS

ACKNOWLEDGMENTS

Special thanks . . .

To Tami Barthel, the one my heart adores a million times over. You've been my closest friend and confidant since I was twenty-two years old. You are the Jonathan to my David. You've always been loyal, faithful, true, and pure. I love you!

To Tammy "Tamster" Dutey. You came to my "Praise Aerobics" classes more than fifteen years ago and have never left my side. Out of all the women who were trained for this hour, you are the one whom I wouldn't have expected to remain. You are both loyal and courageous. I'm forever grateful.

To Mike & Dianna Texter. The day all was stripped away, you offered your home to Brian and me. Dianna, who knew more than twenty-five years ago we would become the closest of sisters? Through your own tragic losses, you have remained faithful. May God raise up those who unselfishly give of their finances to further God's kingdom. Thank you for loving us!

To Michelle Wiklund, a 2 Kings widow who housed, cared for, and loved the prophet only three months after losing your husband. You opened your home, heart, and checkbook. We not only gained a friend but a spiritual mother. Thank you for trusting the God who is in us.

To Cindy Statham-Hestla. Thank you for encouraging me to speak and share stories when all I wanted to do was get to the point. Not only have you been one of my editors, but you have been a true sister. I am able to speak again because of your unconditional love and understanding.

To Jeannie Baye, my assistant, intercessor, and friend. I've never had anyone dream about me on a weekly basis! You're a true servant of the Lord. Thank you.

To my beloved Intercessors. Thank you for selflessly covering me. You are the mid-wives to this game changer!

To all the volunteers. Throughout the years of "Praise Aerobics" to "The Word and the Workout," thank you for selflessly opening up the gyms, setting up, tearing down, doing office work, and assisting me at seminars and conferences. May God remember your servanthood.

To all my spiritual children: Steve, Heather, Crystal, Patrick, and the countless eaglets, God has blessed me with being able to raise you up and mentor you. Remember, no one can stop your destiny but you. Stay focused on Jesus, and only allow voices who believe in you to speak into your life. Draw from each other always!

To Brian "Mr. Unbreakable" Warren. When everyone questioned my motives and left me, God sent you. At the time I thought I was there to save you, but all along it was I who needed saving. When I wanted to retreat inside myself, it was your voice telling me I would save the world. You drew out the warrior within me. She would never have emerged if you had not come along. When during the writing of this book I experienced numerous attacks, and I told you that I am always a problem to everyone who knows me, you said, "You're the best problem anyone could have." You are the closest example on this earth to my relationship with Jesus. I love you, man of God, my husband.

To Jesus, the reason I live, breathe, and have my being. The day you told me I will continue to make mistakes but my mistakes will never make who I am, my perspective changed forever. You're the unconditional example of love that never fails us. You consume me. I asked you many years ago why you would create me with such fire if many people wouldn't want to come near me? You told me that my time would come and they would have to listen. They were not ready then, but they are now! You are a faithful God.

> Who am I, Sovereign LORD, and what is my family, that you have brought me this far? And if this were not enough . . . you have also spoken about the future of the house of your servant. (2 Samuel 7:18-19).

FOREWORD

It is such an incredible honor for me to write the foreword for my beloved amazing friend and true sister of my heart, Prophet Gina Guy-Warren. Prophet Gina is not only one of the most accurate and discerning women I have ever known, but her courage, her tenacity, and her godly ferocity in the Spirit is one of the most unique and rare anointings I have ever encountered. Years of fire and testing have forged Gina into what I believe is one of the most powerful warriors of the Father. She operates faithfully day in and day out as an affront to the kingdom of darkness with a *breaker anointing* that I believe with all my heart will set multitudes free from the shackles and strongholds of the enemy!

The words written in this devotional are saturated with the Zoe life of God, supernatural insight, wisdom, and a *breaker anointing* that will demolish major strongholds in your life. I believe with all my heart that as you read these pages, you will experience divine deliverance, and many years of demonic shackles will be broken over your mind, soul, and emotions. You will experience divine shifting that will bring you into the freedom for which you have been yearning.

Prophet Gina prays unceasingly. Loves unrelentingly. Worships faithfully in the secret place day in and day out. Fights and wars for *you* as Deborah did for her people. She is one of God's unique wonder women in the world today.

Gina, I adore you. It is my greatest honor to call you my friend. I believe with all my heart that this devotional is birthed straight from heaven.

With all my love and respect,
—Wendy Alec
Prophet/Seer, Co-Founder of GOD TV,
Author of The Chronicles of Brothers Book Series

PREFACE

FROM MY HEART: A LOOK BACK AT MY LIFE

Welcome to The Word and the Workout™: a prophetic look into the many dimensions of the spiritual walk as we compare them to natural truths. As I have learned to look back at my own life and examine both patterns and cycles, I can see how connections with people, events, and places have become a road map for my future. When I was sixteen years old I joined a gym for the first time—a gym in Cerritos, California, owned by Rudy and Virginia Smith. When Virginia first noticed me working out, she hired me to teach aerobic classes. Her husband, Rudy, partnered with Jack LaLanne, the creator of the "Smith machine," which is a squat rack that assists in leg workouts. Arnold Schwarzenegger used this machine back in his training days. I was energized the moment my feet stepped into the fitness room, which was filled with people training with weights and taking aerobics classes. The beat of the music exhilarated me, and somehow, I knew I was home. It made sense I would later become the founder of a fitness corporation in addition to a preaching ministry. While working on certifications in various areas of fitness and natural health during my early twenties, I met a woman who opened my eyes to the importance of our colons. I explained to her how the pain medication I was taking was causing constipation. Thus began my amazing journey into natural pathways of healing, where I pursued and received various certifications both in homeopathic medicine and multiple areas of fitness training. I was determined to help others as this woman had helped me. My passion was to preach Jesus and save God's people from religion and medications, while training their bodies emotionally, physically, and spiritually! In 2014 I found myself learning about God's miracle tree, *Moringa oleifera*, through a company called Zija International, which carries the only cell-ready, enzymatically alive *Moringa* on the planet, backed by science! This journey led to meeting Ken Brailsford, the multimillionaire known as the "father of encapsulation"!

If you are familiar with our ministry, you may know that the number 22 is significant for me in many ways. I was born the middle child between two brothers; we were all born twenty-two months apart from each other. I had my first "death walk" dream in 2006, just prior to my divorce, and awoke at 2:22 a.m. This visitation prepared me for the next eight years of single motherhood. I met Brian in 2014, and his fighting number was "Mr. Unbreakable 22." The first property I purchased as a single woman was located on Lot 38222. This number appears throughout my life in various ways.

Now back to my childhood. As the only girl, I found myself competing with the boys in every sport possible. I say *competing*, but every sport in which I participated seemed to require very little effort, as I recognized at a young age that I was in my element. I was even placed on the "Seals" baseball team as the only girl! In 2015 the *Benicia Herald* newspaper in Northern California wrote a front-page article calling Truth-N-Love Ministry the "Navy Seals" of the church.

When I was in my late thirties, I began training Homeland Security personnel from the gym in my garage. Since moving to Tennessee, my husband has been hired as security detail, which connects him with those who work in high-security positions, including the White House. Together we minister to athletes and professionals within the UFC (Ultimate Fighting Champions). While writing this book, I was even reminded of Dennis Tinerino, who won the Mr. Universe title multiple times, as well as Mr. World in 1971. I had the opportunity to meet him when I was eighteen or nineteen years old. He ministered to Tiffany, a popular teenage singer who hit the charts in 1987 with the remake of "I Think we're Alone Now." She had purchased the home of Chuck Norris (actor and creator of Total Gym) in Los Angeles, California, where Dennis held Bible studies that I attended. In 1990 Dennis was diagnosed with cancer and was told he would only live two more years. Amazingly he lived twenty more years and passed away in 2010.

In 2015 I was given a prophetic word concerning three houses being cleaned up. I was told God was pulling the "Trump card," and the White House, Courthouse, and the church house would be cleaned up. The most important house to the Father is His church, so He is saving the best for last!

I write all of this to say that if we pay attention to the road maps of our lives, we will see how everything connects. From the places we have been, to people who come in and out of our lives; every piece fits within the frame of the puzzle. We know in part and we see in part, but as we gather all the "parts" of our journey and begin to put them all in perspective, we will have clearer direction for our futures. I hear so many people say they have no idea what their purpose is and they feel so lost. When I hear their stories, it's easy for me to see their purpose and callings.

If you are someone who feels lost on the battlefield—taking hits left and right, but you don't understand your position—look back! How has the enemy attacked you throughout your life? Were you sexually molested? Were you adopted? Have you gone through a brutal divorce? The Bible tells us our steps are ordered by the Lord; so, if we can look at where we have been, we will have greater understanding of where we are headed! In no way does this mean God causes trauma in our lives, but we can be certain He will use our pain to heal and propel someone else! The vision will get clearer as the blueprint comes into focus. For example, when a contractor draws up the plans to build a home, he starts with the basic framework. The foundation and framing are drawn with the use of tracing paper. Next, the details within the house are added, such as rooms, bathrooms, and square footage. You see where I am going with this. Look back and trace the footsteps of your life, both good, bad, and even what may appear to be inconsequential. All of these details are woven throughout our journey, and we haven't been able to realize it until now! I have applied this wisdom when making decisions concerning God's will for my life. I can't tell you how many times I've been asked how I knew I was to move, or how I knew this or that. Of course, we don't have all the answers, and leaning upon God is first and foremost, but the blueprints are there! We need only to pull out the tracing paper and ask for the dimensions to be revealed. Our lives are not one-dimensional or conclusive. We must seek the one who created our bodies and formed us with intentional purpose!

As I've traced areas of my life, I can see various dimensions attached to the publishing of this book. I can look back at all the events and people I have met and recognize how they helped to fill in the details within the framework of my blueprint.

I was given a vision of standing on a platform with big screens behind me flashing lyrics, phrases, pictures, and words that coordinated with the beat of the music. People filled the conference floor but not with Bibles in hand waiting for the keynote speaker; they were ready to work out! I was leading these sessions filled with godly music and preaching while those who attended were exercising at their individual fitness levels. Some were in wheelchairs, or sitting in chairs holding hand weights, modifying the moves others around them executed at their individual fitness levels. Every ethnic and age group was represented. Not one person was left out, regardless of fitness level, gender, age, or religious beliefs. I saw husbands and wives as well as children attending. This was not your average weekend getaway but something totally different. After the training sessions, the attendees would rest and return for Bible study. I saw the new church rising completely out-of-the-box! I have every hope that you, too, will come to understand your identity and purpose.

We are first sons and daughters in Christ Jesus. Second, titles never define who we are! Always remember: your gifts make room for you, and the Lord will use those gifts to launch your destiny. I pray that you will enjoy your journey as you reflect back on the people, places, and events throughout your life. You, too, will begin to see your purpose and understand a little clearer where your future is headed!

At the end of every devotional, you will see four questions. I encourage you to write your answers, thoughts, and prayers in a separate journal, or at the bottom of each Call to Action page. Be expecting to trace your very own blueprint, as you will, in the details of your destiny!

Gina Guy-Warren

Warriors still exist today.
Their armor has changed.
It's not shiny or impressive.
They are clothed in humility.
Totally unassuming.
Be careful not to overlook them.
They are approaching the frontlines
battle-tested, fierce and loyal.
You're going to need them in this
final hour.

No one can stop a battle in its tracks.
No one who does evil can be saved by evil.

(Ecclesiastes 8:8 MSG)

DAY 1

CAN SOMEONE CALL A DOCTOR?

For the hurt of the daughter of my people am I [Jeremiah] hurt; I go around mourning; dismay has taken hold of me. Is there no balm of Gilead? Is there no physician there? Why then is not the health of my people restored [Because Zion no longer enjoyed the presence of the Great Physician.]

— Jeremiah 8:21-22 AMPC

We all are born with a destiny that only we can fulfill. Once we recognize who we really are, nothing can detour us from our purpose. Although many may seek to "copycat" others, we won't excel in our divine purpose until we get a hold of understanding that our destiny is unique to us. The prophet Jeremiah understood his unique purpose. In our devotional reading you can almost feel the pain within his heart, as he called God's people back to the presence of the Great Physician. These two verses speak volumes to those who want to understand the heart of this prophet. He was bearing a great pain and was burdened within his heart for God's people. The harvest had come and gone, but the false prophets and teachers continued to teach from their own souls, leaving the people with no balm to ease their sadness. Jeremiah assessed the well-being of God's people and concluded, after all had been said and done, they were in worse shape than ever before. You can almost hear him crying out within these passages, "Someone, please call a doctor for these people!" This entire chapter unfolds the false teaching that had spread among His people, leaving them void of healing and ultimately rejecting the true wisdom of God! Jeremiah lamented that the people were looking for peace and completeness but no good came. As a matter of fact, within their search for help, their condition worsened. I share in the plight of this prophet. His heart was hurting for God's people so much; he went about mourning and in dismay. They needed healing and restoration but instead were becoming increasingly ill. Jeremiah asked, "Where is the presence of the Great Physician?"

I don't know about you, but I see history repeating itself. The very purpose and passions that have driven me to write this book are exactly what Jeremiah expressed. False teachers, prophets, and leaders have exchanged the presence of God for the love of money. The accolades and praises of people fuel their messages. In 2 Timothy 3 Paul states:

> People will be lovers of themselves, lovers of money . . . having a form of godliness but denying its power. Have nothing to do with such people.
>
> They are the kind who worm their way into homes and gain control over gullible women. (verses 2, 5-6).

SIMPLY STATED, the body of Christ is ill. Someone has to stop these people from spreading disease! I find it fascinating that Paul used the term "gullible women," because generally women are the ones I see looking for intercession groups on social media or within their local churches. They're the ones viewing and commenting on the "prophet's" videos on social media and crying out for help and answers. Do you suppose that many of these diseases are coming through the social media portals of false teachers? Many people are searching for the presence of God through social media preachers. Personally, I know quite a few believers who are in the midst of abusive marriages, drug addiction, extreme physical handicaps, and experiencing out-of-control demonic activity in their homes. Some are on dating sites where they are being lured into giving away all their retirement savings! I am speaking of believers who go to church! I understand that we are all responsible for our own actions; but the truth is that when people are sick emotionally, physically, and spiritually, their first instinct is to ask someone to prophesy over them, or they make a doctor's appointment for medications, hoping that will cure what ails them. Calling on preachers and doctors before consulting the Great Physician has resulted in unnecessary heartache. Even well-meaning leaders are tolerating these hirelings because it grants them access to the platforms they believe they need to exercise their gifting. Trust me when I tell you that God doesn't need help to launch your destiny. However, as Jeremiah states, God's prophets and pastors will be held accountable for neglecting to expose this *treason* that is infiltrating the church (read Jeremiah 23). Many people enjoy the new "Facebook Live preacher" and what he or she has to say. It is an easy platform for some, not all, charismatic personalities and their heavenly visions to draw thousands of vulnerable followers. Who has qualified these people, and who is testing the spirits coming forth?

In 2010 I found myself mediating a financial scandal between a woman and her pastor. Barry Minkow, the infamous ZZZZ Best Carpet Cleaning mastermind and evangelical-preacher-turned-crime-fighter, had allegedly taken this woman's money. I knew when this meeting took place in my home that God had a serious mission ahead for me, and my hands were full as I counseled and prayed over this man, his wife, and the elders of his church on many separate occasions. I warned him privately numerous times to come clean or God would deal with him publicly. The Spirit of God revealed to me that this pastor was stealing from his flock and having affairs and hiding money in off-shore accounts, all while running the Fraud Discovery Institute out of San Diego Community Bible Church, where he was pastor.[1] Famous directors and actors were launching a new movie about his life of "redemption," while at the same time he was stealing from his congregants and others.[2] Trust me when I tell you this is only a snippet of what took place.

The final straw was when Minkow fled the state of California in the middle of the night, to Tennessee, with his wife and twin boys they had adopted from Guatemala. I had no way of reaching his wife with whom I had become good friends, until she contacted me months later. This sweet woman was still brainwashed and traumatized; but after much counsel, our ministry paid for a divorce attorney on her behalf. We moved her and the boys back to our location in California and assisted her in various ways during the public scandal. I received threats from various influential Christian leaders for supporting this divorce and keeping her in seclusion. I was told God hates divorce and I was out of order. My reply was simply, "God also hates that pastors are paying for breast augmentations for their secretaries while preaching the gospel." Suffice it to say, I didn't hear from them again. This woman was brave and courageous to leave this narcissistic "pastor" whom everyone adored and worshiped. From the Fraud Discovery Institute he ran, to the church, and so much more, Minkow strategically planned all of it to cover up his sin.

Eventually, Barry Minkow was sentenced to five years in federal prison. He pled guilty to a single count of conspiracy related to his issuing a report claiming fraud at Lennar Homes and subsequently placing bets (putting options) that the stock would go down.[3]

I informed the church's lead elder that the break-in at the church, where only the computers were stolen, was executed by their pastor. I was not believed at the time. Barry Minkow has since been ordered by the courts to pay back 3.4 million dollars in restitution to the victims; 2.8 million goes directly to the church. Like so many people in churches today, women feel both trapped and obligated to stay faithful. Someone had to expose this web of deceit, and I did so without reservation!

This is only one story in my journey to fulfill the mandate of God on my life. To say I can relate to the prophet Jeremiah is an understatement. As he declared in our scripture reading, he went about mourning, and dismay had taken hold of him. I, too, will not rest until I see with my own eyes the bride of Christ emerge in purity. Our president will not be the one to save the church. He is not our Savior, and he isn't the answer to the problems in our world—we are! In Isaiah 45:1 we are told that Cyrus was God's chosen instrument to subdue nations before him and unarm and ungird the lions (the pride) of kings. This Cyrus-anointed leader, handpicked by God, was positioned so that the "red tsunami," which is not the politicians but the blood of Jesus, could cover the earth! Underneath this covering, God's warriors are to advance on this earth to take land and territory. We must drain the swamp waters of the church because the Father is more than ready to bring blessing to His beloved bride. Just because someone can prophesy and move in the anointing does not automatically mean he or she earns God's approval. The gifts and call of God are irrevocable (Romans 11:29). One can operate powerfully in God, but his or her character will manifest as well. I believe the two must become one! There is much to learn from the mistakes of leaders, and an infected wound must first be cleansed. Jesus is the author of restoration, and to the degree the devil has come into someone's life, once the wounds have been healed, the power of God will flow through those areas! We must expose infection, not cover it up.

God has you in the palm of His hand, and He is asking you to be patient in your suffering. You may have put all your trust in humans and as a result are suffering deep wounds infected with betrayal. Rest assured He is doing something about it, and He is watching over His Word to perform it. You are His Word, and you are His promise. He called your very life into existence. God hasn't forgotten you; He will restore your hope! Sometimes the con artists are in the congregation, and they leave the pastor and the sheep violated, stripped, and bleeding. It can cut both ways... When the platform (the head or leader) is contaminated, the entire body suffers as a result.

The Great Physician is about to answer your prayers. Get ready to witness restoration, healing, and power as they sweep through the church! He is a God of order, and the trumpet has sounded. Heaven and earth are about to collide, and His righteousness shall be established!

A CALL TO ACTION

- Below or in a separate journal, list the symptoms that you're suffering with emotionally, physically or spiritually.

- Ask the Holy Spirit to reveal their origins (point or place something began).

- List any areas where you have placed your trust in man instead of God.

- Are you in any type of danger?

- **Counseling is available. Contact our ministry for details: Info@tnlmi.org*

DAY 2

THE MIND: WOMB OF INCUBATION FOR EVERY THOUGHT

We demolish arguments and every pretension that sets itself up against the knowledge of God, and we take captive every thought to make it obedient to Christ.

— 2 CORINTHIANS 10:5

Let's begin with the word *incubation.* If we take a moment to break down and comprehend the meaning of this word, we will then be able, once and for all, to win the battle of the mind! I love the word *incubate* because it means "to sit upon . . . for the purpose of hatching," or "to maintain a favorable temperature and in other conditions promoting development as . . . prematurely born infants," or "to develop or produce."[1] Our devotional passage, 2 Corinthians 10:5, is a well-known verse in the walk of many believers, but why are so many people failing at taking our thoughts captive? How does one really capture a thought, and once we capture it, well, what do we do with it? You're reading this book because you desire to commit to a spiritual fitness plan, and you want to succeed not just for a season but also for a lifestyle. We know God's Word will impart wisdom; however, we must also have a plan in order to bring about this desired result.

I hear over and over again from well-meaning believers, "I am going to stand." Well, now that you're standing, it's time to put action to that stand of faith—get up, and move! There comes a time when the body must actually move and put faith into action. Nothing is going to get accomplished just because you're "standing in faith." In reality convincing ourselves that something will happen simply because we believe is a form of passive-aggressive behavior. Enough standing and enough praying! Now let's put into action everything we claim to believe. James 2 is very clear that faith and works must be exercised together: "What is the use (profit), my brethren, for anyone to profess to have faith if he has no [good] works [to show for it]? Can [such] faith save [his soul]?" (verse 14 AMPCE). Notice that James doesn't mention the spirit, but the soul, where three areas can work against us: mind, will, and emotions. Since the apostle Paul warns us to take every thought captive, we had better figure out how to protect our minds. So many books have been written on this subject, I discern that the church house is in desperate need of some serious renovation! I detect a clear and present danger!

Everything in life begins in the mind; we cannot act until thoughts and ideas have first entered into the womb of our minds. This is why Paul explains that both arguments and pretensions are a complete set-up against the knowledge of God. Our past experiences make us who we are today, and many of us have experienced great trauma. When we envision our minds as wombs (an original place of development), then we understand why so many people are unable to remain disciplined in various areas such as workout programs, New Year's resolutions, and, yes, even falling away from the faith (1 Timothy 4:1). *Thoughts are the vehicle in which success or failure travels,* and the final destination is completely up to us. When we travel a road that leads us to our destination, do we not consider the pit stops, rest stops, and everything else along that path? The devil works so hard on our minds because he has a road trip planned for us to derail us—take us off our course—and divide us from each other. Whatever road God places us upon, you can be sure there is someone along that road who needs Him. If we are taken out of position, we miss an opportunity to help another soul. Imagine this: not only do we have the power to pull others to their destinies, but we have the ability to steer them off course as well. I've always said we are positioned for souls!

Thoughts never lie dormant but are fully alive, locked and loaded at all times. I'm reminded of Jeremiah 29:11 where God Himself tells the prophet He already knows (the Hebrew meaning is "to be with us intimately") the thoughts He has towards us, thoughts for good and not evil, for a hope and a future. God's thoughts are always good, pure, true, and stable. He is the only faithful, true, and wise God; therefore, if His thoughts bring about His desired plan for our lives, then we, too, must think on these things. Our thoughts will produce either good results or evil results. Stop and meditate on that for a minute.

Something has gone terribly wrong within the body of Christ, because millions are *not* seeing the fruit of what God Himself has provided for us. Does this mean God is a liar and His word isn't true? Of course not! So, somewhere between God's spoken word and our ability to incubate this word, a terrorist is infiltrating the womb of our minds! When we can identify the terroristic thought, capture it, and insist it obey, then we will begin to see the fruit of God's good plan for us. The Word of God declares, "You have seen correctly, for I am watching to see that my word is fulfilled" (Jeremiah 1:12). He's watching over His Word to perform it. Either God isn't really watching over us, or we haven't learned to (1) think obedient thoughts and (2) protect our thoughts during incubation so nothing foreign or contrary to truth can impact us negatively. Any thoughts that we choose over God's perfect thoughts towards us are sin.

Simply stated, *sin* is any area of our lives over which we have not given Jesus complete authority. We give Him permission and then we take it back over and over. However, I believe understanding the incubation process will assist us in eradicating terroristic thoughts both foreign and domestic! Foreign, meaning negative influences coming from the outside, and domestic, meaning inherited, or sins of the fathers passed down to us. When thoughts contrary to your success enter the womb of your mind, our first thought should be to abort them immediately. Remember, incubating, or providing a favorable condition, for these negative thoughts will give life to those thoughts, allowing them the potential to destroy everything God has intended for both ourselves and those around us. This is the very reason a premature baby is placed in a protective incubator until his or her internal organs are safely developed. A *qualified* physician makes the determination when to release that baby from the incubator. In the spiritual realm many of us are not ready for promotions because our "internal organs" are not developed enough to go to the next level. The Great Physician knows that free radicals (unstable molecules responsible for aging, tissue damage, and possibly some diseases that look to bond with other molecules to destroy their health and cause damage) will attack our minds and take us out of position. He knows whether we have dealt with thoughts and insecurities that attack on the inside and negative influences that assault us from the outside! The best line of defense is reading our Bibles every day. This is God's knowledge concerning our lives. The only way to override the arguments and pretensions within our own minds, wills, and emotions is to replace them daily with God's truth!

We alone are responsible for the way we think about ourselves and others. We can't blame another for our thoughts. The church would flourish and grow exponentially if everyone grasped these incubation concepts. Make certain every thought that comes through your mind today is made a slave to obedience, not evil and disobedience. The Bible is the filter through which everything foreign must pass. The more "fake news," "gloom and doom" prophets, or "candy-coated preaching" we open your minds to, the more they will change who we are. Our own DNA becomes mutated, and the things of this world will defile the purity God desires for us. The more we listen to God's voice, the more knowledge of God we receive. This is the only sure defense we have in these last-day battles that are now upon us.

You're about to receive discharge orders to leave the Intensive Care Unit you have taken residence in for many years. You were not admitted there by the Great Physician because you did something wrong but because you have done everything right! Your internal organs have now matured, and not only does great promotion await you, but the knowledge of God has equipped you to fight all forms of spiritual warfare imaginable! Your ability to demolish every pretension and falsehood setting itself up against God is vital to your survival and that of your family. The times in which we live demand obedience, and obedience begins with controlling our own thoughts. The thoughts you have incubated will be your best line of defense. The degree to which you've incubated godly thoughts, will determine the effectiveness of your defense against the false knowledge that permeates this world and the church.

A CALL TO ACTION

- List any negative or painful thoughts you tend to rehearse on a daily basis.
- Is it possible that lack of forgiveness is the underlying factor?
- What thoughts are you currently incubating (supporting, developing)?
- Find a scripture in God's Word to replace the infectious thoughts.

DAY 3

WHAT IS FOCUSED ANGER?

"Be angry, and do not sin"—do not let the sun go down on your wrath.

— Ephesians 4:26 NKJV

When I married a two-time championship belt holder in the MMA industry, "King of the Cage," let me tell you, I entered the cage as well! Nothing rattles this man, and watching how he handles pressure, resistance, and aggravating situations has taught me quite a bit about self-control and my lack thereof. Gleaning from this legend has caused me to grow in countless areas. Brian tells the story of a time when he was a young boy and was seriously overcome with emotions when he heard his stepfather cry for the first time. Apparently, his stepfather had just lost his own father (Brian's grandfather), but Brian didn't know how to deal with this pain or how to express it. So he ran outside to the backyard and began doing pull-ups until he could no longer pull himself up. He exhausted himself through physical exertion; then he began to weep.

The fruit of these character traits proved to be beneficial when he lost custody of his daughter during his divorce. She had accompanied him on a daily basis to the gym he owned and operated while his wife at the time worked as well. When Brian was served divorced papers, he retained no lawyer but chose to move out of the home they bought when they married, trusting that what his wife had promised him would be carried out. Brian's concern was not his portion of any assets but the shared custody of his daughter. However, when legal documents arrived, Brian was not awarded parental custody and no portion of the equity of their home, leaving his car to eventually become his home.

While Brian was still living in their home with his wife and daughter, he was pumping gas at a local gas station when he spotted a familiar truck he had seen his wife driving pull into the station. Her new love interest got out of the truck and locked eyes with Brian. Now, I need to explain the mind-set of a fighter, soldier, or warrior. These men and women are fiercely loyal to family and country and have an innate gift from God to defend and protect. Anything or anyone that threatens these boundaries is in danger of serious harm or even death. Their minds are constantly rehearsing scenarios as to how to take down an opponent. At this season in Brian's life, he had more than sixty professional fights under his belt. His profession entailed mentally going over takedowns, submission, punching, grappling, and rear naked choke strategies. In the blink of an eye the filmstrip of how to take out this man who "took out" his family flashed across his mind. Brian made his way over to his new opponent. Fear flooded this man as his voice shook, and he said, "Hey, I have no problem with you, man." In that moment Brian had to make a cognitive decision to stand down! Brian replied, "We do have a problem. I cannot change what's up with you and my wife, but do not ever try replacing me as the father of my baby girl!" Brian then got into his car and drove away. He channeled all that anger into his next fight and won two championship belts during that heart-wrenching season.

Brian has fought and trained with some of the best fighters in the world, most of whom are not Christians. How fitting it was that the champions in this industry gave Brian his fighting name "Mr. Unbreakable," not because he has never broken a bone, but because he has proven time and time again that he truly possesses an "unbreakable spirit." He may have been knocked down, but let me tell you something, Brian won't lose the same way twice. He teaches men how to focus their anger in a specific direction, and with God's timing they will arise even greater, stronger, and wiser!

On the day of the confrontation at the gas station, Brian's character collided with the powerful emotion of "anger," and the result was self-controlled focused anger! We must keep in mind that anger is many times the result of unresolved pain. When we suffer betrayals and unjust treatment, we must guard our response. If we do not confront and deal with our pain in due time, our responses can become explosive. This episode at the gas station could have been a disaster for both men. It is interesting it took place at a fueling station, isn't it? Brian could have been fueled by explosive rage, yet instead he chose focused anger.

Anger is so out of control these days, especially as we witness the effects of the current Trump administration in the White House. Beyond a shadow of a doubt, this extreme personality was placed into the position of president of the United States to draw out emotions in everyone: the good, bad, and indifferent! It is working, isn't it! I want to be clear that not one of us is perfect. When Donald Trump entered the race, every character flaw was exposed. We never support sin, but we must continue to pray for the healing of his soul. First Timothy 2:1-4 instructs us to pray for everyone, especially kings and those in authority. Matthew 5:44 says, "But I tell you, love your enemies and pray for those who persecute you." God is calling forth these types of warriors who are so disciplined, nothing and no one can break them or shake them. Again, keep in mind that their experiences in life prepared them for this next level. Brian and I have always said, "Love us or hate us, but one day you're going to need us." Warriors will jump in front of a bullet for you. Danger only fuels purpose in such a person.

President Trump is said to only sleep four hours a night.[1] He is always on watch, and his sole purpose is to "make America great again." He accomplishes this through a warrior mind-set of "take no prisoners." Whatever it takes to flush out the fake, then so be it! President Trump faces evil dictators, fake media, and fake politicians, affording them no ground. He uses every weapon in his arsenal. How many of you, like President Trump, would point at the camera and call those trying to get close to you "fake"? Not everyone who draws close is fake, but when you are made aware of these motives, will you expose them? President Trump's methods may appear to be messy, but he gets the job done and allows no one to take ground against the mission at hand. This is how respect is earned.

In this day and age, especially with the abundance of social media "keyboard warriors," we think nothing of mouthing off to people. We give no thought before posting our harsh opinions or judgments to a leader or about a leader. Here is my famous #quote for those who are so happy to dish out advice but have never gone through the crushing challenge of their positions: #PutAnother-ChickenintheCrockpot. In other words, get your own house in order before you attempt to run someone else's house! (Matthew 7:3-5; Luke 6:41-42).

Respect for others is almost nonexistent these days! I observe people acting as if they are entitled without ever paying any price. It seems that people are losing their minds, approaching others with uncontrollable emotions and lashing out with no concern of retaliation. We are living in a time where it's perfectly acceptable to accuse reputable men of serious crimes, including sex crimes, but present zero evidence. We have become a society of "guilty until proven innocent," instead of the other way around. On the other hand, rapes and pedophilia are occurring within churches, while leadership conveniently covers up the crime and blames the victim. We see leaders stealing mantles, ministries, and sheep from one another, and friends betraying friends. I offer two simple reasons why all this is going on. First, we have lost the fear and reverence for God. He has become our best friend and hangout buddy. He smokes and drinks with us while we are backstabbing our fellow soldiers with our words and actions.

We engage in adultery on Saturday night and sing in church on Sunday. Second, there are no consequences for the offender. As a church we tolerate and love, but we are afraid to hold people accountable for their actions. We totally disregard Matthew 18:15-17, where Jesus taught about dealing with offenders in the church.

I have heard people say, time and time again, "Leave it in God's hands," and "He is the one who will judge and convict." Can you imagine our president approaching evil dictators with this type of passive attitude? He is able to drain the swamp waters because of his courage, and he is not afraid to act. How is it that we display zero fear after stealing another man's wife or shamelessly spreading rumors and gossip?

The spirit of a true warrior is to be reverently feared. Mark my words! The men and woman who are rising up now will be a clean-up crew, making a way for the pure in heart who desire to glorify God in all they do. Jesus Himself is a mighty warrior, and we are about to see our Warrior and Defender arise on behalf of all His children who are being accosted! How will He accomplish the cleaning of the church house? By gathering His wounded warriors who have learned to turn their pain into purpose! They hold a sharp double-edged sword in their hands. On one side is written the names of every spirit that has been assigned to attack them. On the other side is written, "Victory!" Their grip is firm, and they are not afraid to perfectly wield this sword. They have become expert sword persons who take out the enemy, not each other.

Anger is not a sin nor is it a weakness! When focused in the right direction, anger can be your greatest weapon to use against the hordes of hell. Your loving Father, in His eternal wisdom, has allowed Sergeant Pain, Sergeant Disappointment, and Sergeant Betrayal to drill you in this boot camp called Life. God is training you for a high-level position in His special ops. You are His secret weapon!

A CALL TO ACTION

- Have you been told your emotions are sinful?
- Do you have anger issues that are controlling you now? How can you refocus them?
- Are there some areas you find yourself wanting revenge or pay back?
- How can you diffuse an angry environment with a family member or co-worker?

DAY 4

THE FIRE IS KINDLED: WILL YOU FOLLOW AT A DISTANCE?

Seizing him [Jesus], they led him away . . . Peter followed at a distance. And when some there had kindled a fire in the middle of the courtyard and had sat down together, Peter sat down with them.

— LUKE 22:54-55 NIV

Approximately fifteen years ago, while I was in my prayer time, I was given a vision. To this day it shines as vividly as it did the day I received it. As I was reading our scripture verse for the day and saw the word *kindled*, this vision popped to the forefront of my mind: I was sitting with Jesus next to a campfire. Other people were in this circle, but they were unidentifiable. It was a dark evening, and all I could see was the campfire and Jesus. I was sitting to His right. He turned and asked me a question, "Gina, do you love Me?" I answered without pause, "Yes. You know I love You." He replied, "Then feed My sheep." Jesus then turned to the person sitting next to me, but I had no idea who the person was. He asked, "Do you love Me?" The person responded, "Yes. You know I love You." Jesus replied, "Then take care of My sheep." I recognized what was taking place because I was familiar with John 21, where Jesus restored Peter after he had publicly denied Him. The vision continued as Jesus addressed every person sitting around the campfire. Not one of us knew who else was present because we each felt as if we were the only one there with Jesus. Then something happened. The fire rose and blazed so brightly that every face was revealed in its light, and we could also hear the names being spoken!

Everyone who has surrendered their lives to Jesus can place themselves in the very position Peter found himself in Luke 22. Let's take a look at the scenario so we, too, can learn from Peter's mistake! Judas had already betrayed Jesus. The deceiver-betrayer-Trojan-horse was already in position. Judas had made his way into the inner circle, unidentified for a time, with the other disciples. The religious leaders had seized Jesus, and it was time see who would stand with Him, "but Peter followed at a safe distance" (verse 54). There was a fire kindled in the courtyard, and some townspeople who were out and about sat down to warm up. A servant girl was the first to recognize Peter by the firelight and pointed at him. I can hear her now with a loud voice, "There he is! This man was with Him!" Two others pointed at Peter, agreeing that he is one of the disciples, but all three times Peter denied even knowing Jesus (verses 55-60).

I would like to turn our attention toward the fire in the courtyard, because when I saw "kindled" I was brought back to my vision. The definition of *kindle* is "to cause to glow" or "stir up," as in kindling feelings or interest. It can also mean "to bring forth young."[1] In other words, I believe the kindled fire was a foreshadowing of the Holy Spirit, who would live within the hearts of every person who chooses to accept Jesus Christ as his or her Lord and Savior! This new birth within us would both light up and expose every truth, as well as all deception!

John 14 declares another Counselor would come to be with us forever—the Spirit of Truth. The Holy Spirit teaches us all things and reminds us of every lesson Jesus, or Truth, has spoken to us. We cannot run from truth, for it chases down everyone; but whether or not we choose truth is completely up to us. We have been given a free will to choose, and that's the beauty of Christianity. It is not a forced religion or practice, but rather each individual is presented with the truth of Jesus Christ and may choose it or not. However, I fear most have become too comfortable with this idea and believe recklessly that Jesus will pop up in the nick of time to hear their deathbed confession, so they have plenty of time to consider all their options and course correct along the way.

Let me present what I believe is happening now, as many people are missing what's taking place right before their eyes. I think we can all agree we are living in times where right appears to be wrong, and wrong appears to be right. Of course, this isn't seen only in the political arena. But do you suppose God could be using the White House, and the one He chose to clean it up, to kindle the fire and shed light on the true condition and position of humanity's commitment to Christ? Please allow me to explain. When I stood publicly for President Trump, it didn't take long to see where others stood. I've witnessed people taking one of three positions, and it will be the third one that ties into this devotional. There are those who are either 100 percent on the side of President Trump and those who are 100 percent against him. But my concern is regarding the third position. There are many people out there like Peter who are following at a safe distance! During the course of writing this book, I've lost friends and I've lost family. I've also noticed a group who choose to remain at a safe distance to see how this all works out for *me*. As a matter of fact, I taught a message on tormenting dreams, just like Pilate's wife, who warned him not to crucify Jesus. I have been given countless dreams about those who are neither 100 percent for me nor 100 percent against me but are choosing, rather, to follow at a safe distance. Peter made the same mistake, and I believe it's important for us to learn from it. During the stressful hours after Jesus' arrest, Peter sought comfort beside a warm kindled fire, and it was within the light of this fire, that his true position was illumined. Three days later, just as in my vision, Jesus gave His disciples ample one-on-one time to answer His questions. May I remind you that His questions were not about how we would serve Him, but rather if we were willing to take care of, feed, and love His sheep! You see, if we truly love and obey Jesus at all costs, then out of the overflow of this love we will care for His sheep! It's never the other way around! If all our love and devotion is to Him first, then we will take care of His sheep and be willing to sacrifice our own safety, reputation, and pride!

Our ministry receives countless emails, and many contain the same underlying message: "We follow you and watch all your videos and teachings. We just can't 'like' or share them because others are watching us." Believe me when I say I love receiving these precious messages, but the message in our devotional today plays in my spirit every time I read one of these correspondences. How many believers are choosing to follow at a safe distance when those of us in leadership and authority are choosing to place our reputations on the line to publicly stand with God's plans and purposes?

I also think of the scripture in Matthew 10, "Whoever denies Me before men, I will also deny before my Father who is in heaven" (verse 33 NKJV). I am not saying I am Jesus, nor is President Trump, but what if we are following Jesus and are in a position to lead others to their destinies? To deny is one thing, but I must issue a stern warning for those who are following at a safe distance. Peter was publicly embarrassed because he once stood in the midst of the one and only wise God, prayed and ate with Him, witnessed the miracles and the beatings, and then backed off to a place he hoped would be a safe distance. Guess what? A believer is never in a safe place when he or she has been enlightened to the truth and has walked in the presence of God but backs off when times get tough. Hebrews 6:4 says, "It is impossible for those who have once been enlightened, who have tasted the heavenly gift, who have shared in the Holy Spirit, who have tasted the goodness of the word of God and the powers of the coming age and who have fallen away, to be brought back to repentance. To their loss they are crucifying the Son of God all over again and subjecting him to public disgrace."

Without a doubt, the kindness of the Lord leads to repentance. He has been graciously kind and patient with all of us. He has granted each of us an ample amount of time to follow truth and stand boldly with Him and with those who are representing Kingdom purpose in these final hours. The fire is now kindled! We will all see our hearts and motives exposed in this season and we will know who is within our inner circle. You are either a Judas or a disciple; there is no middle ground! Remember, it was a servant girl, not a "church member" who first exposed Peter as a follower of Christ. The world is watching, and they will not be fooled.

God's people are marked for a great purpose. We must choose to follow Him so closely that we take hold of the hem of His garment. *His power will keep us even when others leave us.* It's a choice we all must make. If you're watching and waiting for Jesus—the Way, the Truth, and the Life—to appear, then you must understand He is sending those first who will be used to kindle the fire before His return! The religious leaders may have seized and accused Jesus falsely, but He now sits at the right hand of His Father, because His Father was the only one Jesus cared to please. Don't be a man pleaser like Peter. Stop being so concerned about guarding your reputation, because when it's all said and done, and you're standing before the Father, it doesn't matter who believed and supported you. Let's learn from Peter's mistake of following at a safe distance, and let's choose today to close that gap!

A CALL TO ACTION

- What are some issues the Holy Spirit has been dealing with you one-on-one?
- List any fears you have related to these issues.
- List the benefits that will outweigh those fears.
- How will you move forward to take a stand publicly for Jesus?

DAY 5

LIONS VS. HYENAS: THE WAY OF A WARRIOR

After that, you may go back and occupy your own land.

— Joshua 1:15

My favorite subject all throughout my schooling was English, so it makes sense that I pay close attention to specific words and how they are used or where they are placed when I read the Bible. I fully enjoy studying Greek, Hebrew, and the etymology of words. Notice that our scripture for today begins with "after," which is a preposition. A prepositional phrase is a group of words used in close connection to nouns and pronouns. When I was shown this specific verse in Joshua 1, I began to search out what the Holy Spirit wanted me to *really* see. After studying the passage, I understood I was reading strategy that would unfold in 2019! I began to understand that this very chapter, which we have most likely read numerous times, contained answers to many problems that exist within the church today. When I read the phrase, "After that," I naturally wanted to know what actions preceded the phrase and who was involved. I was being shown a promise for who would occupy our own land, and I set out to figure out just how that was actually going to happen. Was land just miraculously going to be handed down to us or was there a strategy that needed to be implemented in order to take back land and then occupy?

This devotional reading was inspired by a two-minute clip I viewed on YouTube titled "Lion attacked by pack of hyenas"[1] (I encourage you to view the video clip along with this devotion for even greater understanding). Prophetically speaking, we are in a time of great transition. However, as we shift into new positions of influence, God's strategy must be recognized, embraced, and implemented. Many believers are claiming new land and territory that they believe God has promised they will occupy in 2019, but if we do not heed the wisdom outlined in the book of Joshua, we will not receive these promises. We are not entertaining stories about great warriors in the Bible so we can walk away saying, "Wow, what a great miracle that Joshua delivered everyone into their new land!" But after reading this warrior miracle, we are left feeling defeated, wishing this could be our own personal story. Well, not only *can* it be your story, but it *will* be if you walk out the revelation.

As we read about the baton being passed from the pastor (Moses) to the warrior (Joshua), it would behoove us to be wise and pay attention to *how* victory was obtained. Keep in mind, we can declare and decree until the cows come home; but before these promotions can take place, we must implement the strategy for success as outlined for us in Joshua. If we choose to simply sit around and claim promises, then we will not occupy our land.

Moses has passed away, and Joshua is standing before the very people Moses led out of Egypt. The pastor will always lead you out of Egypt (sin and worldly thinking), but the warrior will annihilate the clear and present danger and then call you forward so you can occupy blessing. The Lord speaks to Joshua and assures him that no one will be able to stand up against him. As He was with Moses, so He shall be with Joshua (Joshua 1:5-6). Land has been promised to the Israelites, and they made it out of Egypt, but now they find themselves waiting to occupy all they had traveled so far to obtain. Joshua, having heard from God Himself, now instructs his commanding officers to go and tell the people to gather their supplies and get ready, because in three days they would occupy! (verses 6-11). Now Joshua addresses the warriors: Reubenites ("ones who see"); Gadites ("invades"); and the half-tribe of Manasseh ("forgets pain associated with trauma"). Joshua tells them the Lord their God is giving them rest and has granted them this land. They are then instructed to leave their wives, children, and livestock behind, everything of value, because these fighting men, fully armed, must cross ahead of their brothers! (verses 12-14a). I would like to direct your attention to Joshua's next statement. Specific instructions are being issued by their new commander and chief warrior, Joshua: "You are to help [your brothers] *until the LORD gives them rest . . . until they too have taken possession of the land*" (verses 14b-15, italics mine). Enter the prepositional phrase I spoke of in the beginning, "After that, you may go back and occupy your own land." These warriors will not occupy their own visions and dreams until they help their own brothers! *BAM!* When can they stop helping their brothers? Only when they see their warriors are at rest and occupying the land they have been fighting to acquire!

Now let's talk about the "Lion attacked by pack of hyena" video I mentioned. The lion in the video was appropriately named "Red." As *he matured*, he would venture out alone to survey the land. One day, exhausted, Red found himself cornered by twenty hyenas. These scavengers circled around him howling and taking bites out of his flesh until they wore him out. Once Red was weak, these hyenas planned to make their final move and pounce all at once to take him out. All of a sudden, another lion appeared because he heard a commotion. Now Red had an ally! When Red's ally appeared, the hyenas backed down because they knew they could not overtake two lions!

We can learn from this video because there are many dimensions of truth displayed. First, I'd like to break down the characteristics of a warrior so we can better understand the instruction we are being given in Joshua 1. Warriors possess an innate God-given desire to venture outside the lines as they begin to mature. They will choose to test the limits and boundaries, regardless of the cost. I've always said that our greatest gifts can also be our greatest areas of weakness. Just like Red, warriors will venture out alone and survey the land; but when a warrior isolates himself, some of the fiercest demonic attacks surround him! It's important to interject here that we must never judge the courage of a warrior because there are more who tend to choose the familiar because it's safe and comfortable. For example, some warriors never leave the cities where they grew up and went to school. Some choose to remain close to people, places, or things because it's safe (or at least they believe this to be true). Those who remain within the boundaries of safety zones will never understand the risk-taking faith of a warrior.

Second, warriors will hold their position even when surrounded by danger. Their first instinct is to fight to the finish until they are either worn down, weak, or have lost their lives to their assailant. They are natural protectors and will never run back to their tribe unless they carry "Goliath's head" in their hands. Defeat isn't an option, and they will not return until they can show victory to their comrades. This isn't pride; it is the confidence and fire within a warrior! Warriors will die before they turn tail and run away from danger. Hence, the very reason many Christian Americans don't understand why President Trump won't back down to our enemies. Even more so, why it "appears" he's not being loyal to America's allies. But, alas, the way of a warrior isn't always understood by the masses. Don't judge what you don't understand or carry within yourself. The lack of understanding these days only illuminates the separation between warriors and civilians. It's inevitable that warriors will face danger and be surrounded by many enemies. Alone, they can only keep their enemies at bay for a while and cannot take them all down at once. Even for a warrior, a certain number of attacks will at some point become too many. Joshua 23:10 declares, "One of you routs a thousand, because the LORD your God fights for you." Deuteronomy 32:30 tells us, "How could one man chase a thousand, or two put ten thousand to flight?"

Now for a brief look at the ways of the enemy. As I viewed the video clip, the hyenas were making irritating screeching sounds and causing confusion as they circled Red. Hyenas are scavengers and eat the leftovers of the one who did all the work. They travel in packs and will operate even in cyclical patterns. Their voices are rarely raised alone. They are cowardly and have to bring someone along to fight their battles. Many of our warriors, both in the military and within the body of Christ, have suffered from PTSD (post-traumatic stress disorder). Our soldiers returning from war are a prime example of this. They have experienced great trauma (like depicted in the video) and have returned home, only to be completely misunderstood.

One by one the body of Christ is being picked off by the enemy. Joshua gave the command to just the warriors, not to all the Israelites! His instructions were to take care of them *until* they were rested and in their land! Why are we so scattered, joining this prayer group, giving to that ministry, attending a different church, and then we move onto the next? Imagine what we would accomplish if our commitments were focused strategically and we remained committed to one ministry or person. *After that* we will occupy our own territories and be at rest.

A CALL TO ACTION

- List one short-term goal and one long-term goal you'd like to accomplish.
- What are some activities, habits, or voices that are distracting or hindering you from achieving these goals?
- Who or what are you committed to at this time?
- Make a list of practical steps that will help you keep these commitments

DAY 6

MOUTH-TO-MOUTH COMBAT: WINNING THE FIGHT

How sweet are your words to my taste, / sweeter than honey to my mouth!

— Psalm 119:103

I get so excited about this particular subject because I know if this book had been released when I first began writing it in the late '90s, the impact would not have been the same as it will be in this very hour! The terms *combat*, *Al Qaeda*, and *terrorists* were not such key words to the average civilian back then; but, sadly, in the times we now find ourselves living, we understand the meanings are quite relevant. When I think of the scripture reading for today, mouth-to-mouth combat comes alive in a whole new light. We understand that the U.S. Department of Homeland Security protects us from internal threats to our nation, and we are taught to apply specific precautions in order to be safe. We are instructed to always be aware of our surroundings and to report suspicious bags or packages at airports or public locations. Yet the very terrorists that have access to us on a daily basis are camped out in our own pantries and refrigerators. They are not external threats but dangers within our own homes. Now that's a real internal threat we have the power to stop! Homeland Security seeks to protect our nation, but who is protecting our families within our own homes? We must get back to basics. There is so much data and nutritional information available, when applied, will save our lives. The *key* word here is "applied," because we can read and listen to every teaching known to man yet find ourselves spiritually constipated. Unless we actually apply what we learn, the results can be catastrophic. I have full confidence that many of you reading this book will be set free by the wisdom and instruction written within its pages. Until we can fully comprehend our behaviors, we will never be able to make wise choices. Isn't it about time we experience complete freedom from our appetites? Never should our flesh dictate any of our actions; however, I see the flesh rule on a day-to-day basis in so many. The term *foodie* is giving license to eat whatever gourmet foods our flesh desires. We shouldn't begin to blame or condemn ourselves but rather make a cognitive effort from this moment on to move forward with insight that will begin to change our habits. To know we can be free from our stomachs ruling our actions is an exhilarating thought! Only when we expose the root cause as to why we make the choices we do, then and only then can we change our behavior patterns. "If the Son sets you free, you will be free indeed" (John 8:36). How can we truly be free unless we understand the underlying force behind certain appetites that control us and cyclical patterns that grip us? Our devotional reading declares that God's words are sweet to our taste, sweeter than honey to our mouths. Hopefully we have friends around us who love reading their Bibles, and like honey, His word glides from their lips. However, it's not difficult to discern those who don't read His Word. I've always said the spiritual has a twin in the natural. When we choose to pay attention to what others speak, we will be made aware of what they choose to "eat" every day.

This scripture came to life when I recommended Zija© Supermix to a client at a local gym. He was at least one hundred pounds overweight. I was thrilled when he received his first order! However, the next time I saw him approaching the gym he had "that look" on his face. Not one person had ever expressed that they didn't like the taste of this 100 percent enzymatically alive *Moringa oleifera*. I encourage every one of my training and counseling clients to take this nutrient. When I explain that by adding one sachet to eight ounces of water, they are flooding their bodies with ninety-two cell-ready nutrients, forty-six antioxidants, thirty-six anti-inflammatories, and eighteen amino acids, it should be a no brainer, right? Not only did he say he didn't like the taste, he went on to say it was the worst thing he had ever tasted! Immediately, the Holy Spirit gave me wisdom that he has been catering to his appetite with all types of junk food and sugar; therefore, his taste buds must be retrained. I understood he was flooding his taste buds with unclean food. Sadly, he was unable to press through, and he gave into the flesh. Proverbs 27:7 uses the term "satiated [with sensual pleasures]," meaning desiring to the point of overindulgence. As Scripture indicates, we will not be hungry for the pure things of God when we continually feast upon the tastes of the world. Please keep in mind; it's no coincidence it can take up to forty days to retrain our taste buds!

Now, let's take a look at the definition of the word *combat*. It means "active fighting especially in a war."[1] We live in a combat zone every single day of our lives with regard to food choices; advertising can seduce and trigger us if we allow it! We are a people drawn by what we see, and some of us fully understand that we will not end up in a place of sin or wrong choices without first thinking about it, then visualizing it. When we watch television commercials or pass by billboards and take in information, we are then triggered in some way. We walk into the grocery store and spot a bag of cookies and begin contemplating if we should buy them. First we look, then we pick them up to consider, right? Without realizing it we entered into a combat zone, and the tasty challenger we now face has the power to take us out, unless we are armed with knowledge, which is wisdom applied! I choose to not take a second glance, because if I do, I may start making excuses and giving myself permission to grab a bag. Do you know that a chemical in these cookies merges with the pleasure center, or nucleus acumens, in your brain, and the addiction is compared to that of cocaine? No addict willingly snorts or shoots up cocaine with the intention of using for the rest of their lives. However, once triggered and activated, the response to cookies is the same as the response to cocaine and morphine!

We all operate from our five senses whether we realize it or not. We are stimulated by what we see, feel, hear, smell, and taste. If we choose to not taste hot dogs, cookies, cakes, and chips, then we can't be seduced. Free will is a force to be reckoned with, isn't it? Some may accuse me of being too religious, but I choose what to put in my body. We are surrounded by chemicals and pollution; and while we don't have a choice what we breathe outside our homes, we do when it comes to what we put in our mouths. We must educate ourselves about GMO's (genetically modified organisms). These organisms are plants and animals that have had their DNA specifically engineered in a way that does not occur in nature. Monsanto, along with other companies, is genetically modifying corn and other foods in order to keep insects from eating them.[2] Makes sense, doesn't it? The farmers lose money when pests consume their crops, and pesticides can be costly. So, why not alter the DNA just enough to repel the bugs? Newsflash! If the bugs are repelled from eating it, why aren't we? The term *genetically modified organism* alone should spur caution because the FDA is attempting to enhance nutrition profiles. Are you aware that one method of inserting the new gene involves using a gene gun? [3] We must educate ourselves regarding just how scientifically modified our food has become. My intention is for you to understand that if you eat food that has been enhanced by "outside sources," then over time you will take on the characteristics of what you eat. (This is partially to blame for the gender confusion infiltrating our society).[4,5] We are taking the "gun" into our own hands and shooting disease-causing chemicals into our own bodies. Dear Lord, what are we thinking, or not thinking, every time we buy so-called food for ourselves and our families!

Let's compare this concept to the spiritual state of the body of Christ today! Preachers are modifying the Word of God to fit their own agendas and belief systems. They inject feel-good messages and plenty of jokes during their sermons, keeping away the pests whom I call truth seekers! We are producing a genetically modified army for Christ that will be powerless to withstand the coming opposition. These soldiers are both confused and suffering identity crises. We are rejecting what is healthy on every level! Our five senses should be awakened, not put into a spiritual coma. Only unfiltered, raw truth can combat lies and gird us up with pure strength! Outside forces are infiltrating us both in the natural and supernatural, but we can choose what we allow to tempt our minds and bodies. If you look in the mirror you will see the direct result of your choices, both good and bad, since the Bible tells us a mirror reflects what's on the inside. (James 1:23). The scripture reading for today cannot sum this subject up any clearer! Our sensual nature wants what's easy and a quick fix, but that has proven to be a danger to the body as a whole. Just like the man who was repulsed by the taste of the Supermix™, people will spit out the natural because they have constantly been feeding on the counterfeit. It's my passion and mission from God to feed the body of Christ with The Word and the Workout prophetic insight into physical, emotional, and spiritual fitness. Let's flood our bodies, minds, and spirits with good things because that is the only way we will overcome evil! We alone are responsible for securing our own homeland, our families!

*FREE COUNSELING IS available on all Zija© orders. See the Appendix for more information.

A CALL TO ACTION

- How often do you read your Bible? Determine a set time each day to read.

- Make a list of items from your pantry and refrigerator and ask the Lord to reveal "terrorists." Replace each item with one healthy food.

DAY 7

VERTICALLY CHALLENGED: EXTRA EFFORT PAYS OFF

There was a man named Zacchaeus, who was a chief tax collector, and he was rich. And he sought to see who Jesus was, but he could not because of the crowd, for he was of short stature.

— Luke 19:2-4 NKJV

Get ready, get set, *and grow*! Have you ever heard someone being described by his or her height, especially in the case of a criminal investigation? The first questions asked of the witnesses are: "What did he look like? How tall was he?" Today's devotional is for everyone who has been defined by physical attributes. In some way or another you've been hindered by what others have viewed as shortcomings.

When we read the story of Zacchaeus, we see him defined by three characteristics. He was *a chief tax collector*, he was *rich*, and he was *short*. He is described negatively as a tax collector but also rich and short, as if these are terrible attributes. Certainly in Zacchaeus's day, his profession was not embraced because tax collectors took everyone's hard-earned money. Added to that, he was rich and also short. For a man I really doubt this description was a confidence builder; but for all those who judged him, it was about to get real up in here! Jesus had entered Jericho and was passing through with no plans to stay. Zacchaeus had heard He was coming and was determined to do whatever he had to do because he didn't want to miss the opportunity to see Him.

I can picture Zacchaeus navigating through the sea of people, standing on the tips of his toes, jumping up and down, and trying his best to see above all the taller men in the crowd. Realizing he is completely hindered because of his height and the size of the crowd, this method of attempting to see Jesus isn't working for him. Instead of giving up, he finds a way. He decides to bypass the crowd by running ahead, anticipating Jesus's route. He finds a sycamore (or fig) tree and climbs it all the way to the top. Now, what happens next is vitally important because when Jesus arrives at that very tree, He looks up! In the midst of this large crowd of people surrounding Jesus, someone catches his attention. Are you aware of how many scripture passages encourage us to look up? For example, Psalm 121:1 says, "I lift up my eyes to the mountains— / where does my help come from?" But Jesus intentionally looks up in that tree knowing Zacchaeus is there. What happens next is nothing "short" of amazing! Jesus speaks directly to Zacchaeus, calling him by name, "Zacchaeus, come down immediately. I must stay at your house today" (Luke 19:5 NKJV).

I can imagine the look on this tax collector's face as he shimmies down that tree, invited to stand right next to Jesus. No more jumping up and down and straining to get a glimpse of the prophet from a distance. They are now face to face! Zacchaeus's ambition, drive, and calculated efforts land him not only in Jesus's presence but with an opportunity to host Him for dinner! No one ever wanted to hang out with Zacchaeus before, let alone go to his home. He's the sinner who takes everyone's money for a living. And, obviously, he must be doing something underhanded because he is rich. All rich people must be ungodly sinners, right? As he and Jesus walk together towards Zacchaeus's home they can hear the crowd mocking and gossiping. (The same crowd that once judged Zacchaeus is the same crowd hurling insults and jealousy because Jesus chose to walk with him).

The kind of tree Zacchaeus climbed is important because the prophetic symbolism is profound truth we must grasp for ourselves. This sycamore, or fig tree, has wide spreading branches and affords delightful shade. It's usually planted by the waysides, and its leaves are heart shaped, downy on the underside, and fragrant. The fruit grows directly from the trunk in little sprigs and clusters like grapes. To make the fruit edible, each one, three or four days before gathering, is punctured with a sharp instrument or fingernail. In 1 Chronicles 27:28 we read that David valued these trees so much he appointed a special overseer for them! What an incredible insight as we see a man who was despised and hated in his community, simply because of his wealth and profession, choose such a tree in order to not miss his time of visitation. Once this guest of honor was in his home, what transpires next unfolds the character of Zacchaeus and why Jesus chose to alter his plans just for this man.

Zacchaeus stands next to Jesus and says, "Lord, I give half of my goods to the poor; and if I have taken anything from anyone by false accusation, I restore fourfold" (Luke 19:8 NKJV). Jesus doesn't even respond to the money issue but says to him, "Today salvation has come to this house, because he also is a son of Abraham; for the Son of Man has come to seek and to save that which is lost" (verses 9-10 NKJV).

Whatever physical limitations or weaknesses have hindered you will now be the very shortcomings that will launch you into great destiny. We must learn to use what we ourselves or others describe as a disadvantage and use it to our advantage. This is the heart and mind of a warrior. Limitations are to be pressed through, not surrendered to.

A little effort pays off, as we witnessed with Zacchaeus. Everything and everyone that could come against him did, but he ran! He ran ahead of everyone. Zacchaeus didn't hang with the crowds or associate with the Who's Who of Jewish society; therefore, he was not welcomed or accepted. He endured jealousy because of his profession and wealth. You may find yourself in the same place as our brother Zacchaeus. However, you cannot allow what you look like, your social status, financial bracket, or anything else to be the defining factor in your relationship with Jesus. On the contrary, it's the foolish things of the world that confound the wisdom of the wise (1 Corinthians 1:27). Zacchaeus embodied the very heart of Jesus. He was ambitious, wise, and determined (who thinks to run to a tree and climb to the top in order to see Jesus?). The most important thing to note from all we read about this tax collector is the one character trait that stands out above all else: he was a giver! This man was judged by his outside appearance, and from that people made a determination that he was a sinner. Surely, he stole from others to become this wealthy. But while others gave 10 percent, Zacchaeus purposed to give Jesus half! His response to Jesus gives us insight into the very heart of this man: *If I have wronged anyone, I will give even more in order to make restitution.*

What can we learn from this unpopular tax collector? Obviously, Zacchaeus's attitude change impressed Jesus, because Jesus's reply was that salvation had come to his house. He even referenced God's covenant with Abraham, to whom He promised that his descendants would outnumber the stars. Massive blessing came to the house of Zacchaeus. A man who wanted to see Jesus pushed beyond what everyone else was doing in order to reach Him. A man who ran ahead and climbed what was the most fruitful, heart-shaped, deeply rooted shade tree in order to see truth from a higher perspective was a rich man with a heart to give more! The end result was that Jesus decided to change His plans and stay in Zacchaeus's home! Salvation and blessing were the result. A little extra effort will pay off, and who knows but blessing and salvation may come to your house this year as well!

A CALL TO ACTION

- In what ways have you been stereotyped throughout your life?
- How have you allowed nicknames and/or stereotypes to limit things you wanted to try?
- List ways you can use those things to your advantage instead of allowing them to hinder you.
- List a few things you would like to revisit. Put a plan in place to accomplish them.

DAY 8

EXERCISING AND EXORCISING LEAPING DEMONS

The possessed man went berserk—jumped the exorcists, beat them up, and tore off their clothes. Naked and bloody, they got away as best they could.

— Acts 19:16 MSG

"My daddy preached the Word of God and cast out demons, so it must be my call as well." Have you ever heard a pastor speak this from the pulpit his father once occupied? Or maybe you feel the pressure of stepping into the position one of your parents once held? I believe what you're about to read will not only give you pause to think twice about stepping into another person's mantle, but it will also drive home the importance of hearing from God on your own behalf. As I've always said, "Stay in your own lane;" because when we step into a place that we were never called to be, we can expect warfare we were never intended to encounter!

Here is the backstory for today's devotion. The apostle Paul had traveled to Ephesus where he met some disciples (Acts 19:1). It's important to note these were *disciples*, followers of Jesus Christ, not unbelievers. Paul proceeded to ask these believers if they had received the baptism of the Holy Spirit. I love how the disciples responded, because it gives us insight into their innocence regarding this subject. They began to explain to Paul that they had never heard of the Holy Spirit. Perplexed, the Great Apostle asked them what type of baptism they had received. The disciples explained they had been baptized by John the Baptist. John's baptism was one of repentance, and they had turned from their old ways and received salvation through Jesus Christ. They had not heard there was another baptism, one that would endow them with supernatural power! (verses 2-3). Paul then explained that there's more to this salvation, and it's called the baptism of the Holy Spirit! Paul then laid hands on them and prayed. One by one they were filled with the Spirit of God and began to speak in tongues and prophesy (verses 4-6).

How thrilling it is to be empowered from within to such a degree that we manifest God's supernatural power, displaying signs and wonders to the world! In other words, these disciples were enjoying sharing the truth of the Messiah with their followers, but it wasn't until the apostle Paul had laid hands upon them that power exploded from the inside out, instead of from the outside in. This added an entirely new dimension to their ministry. These believers were now experiencing in power what they knew in word.

As we continue to read these events in context, we see Paul entering the synagogue and preaching with boldness. However, the religious leaders were obstinate and unbelieving. Paul then chose to leave the synagogue and spent the next two years sowing truth into these twelve men. His mentorship prepared the men to preach the Word with truth and boldness throughout the province of Asia, to both the Jews and the Greeks (verses 8-10).

But I want to give a word of caution, because here comes trouble! Where true anointing and supernatural power is strong and active, you will also find gangs of evil spirits ready to find a body to overpower. We must understand that it is *unexercised*, weak faith that these demonic powers search out. In the physical, when we have an injury to a body part, that part will be the most vulnerable and susceptible to increased attack. The medical term is *atrophy*. Atrophy is the "gradual loss of muscle or flesh usually because of disease or lack of use."[1] Keep this term in mind as we continue our story! While Paul and his disciples were seeing success *exercising* their authority in the name of Jesus and *exorcising* the evil spirits they encountered, there were also other Jews who witnessed this power and tried their hands at it but experienced a completely different result, including the seven sons of a chief priest named Sceva. These men had witnessed the miracles Paul and his disciples were performing and wanted to get in on it (verses 11-14). I can hear them now: "Hey, these guys aren't the only ones who can *exercise* and *exorcise* demons! Besides, our dad's a chief priest; we've got this." But it was time for a reality check! These young men were about to learn the hard way that demons can *exercise* too and physically attack where they sense weakness. Sceva's sons were feeling pretty confident, calling out evil spirits in Jesus's name and seeing good results, but one day a certain evil spirit actually talked back. Let's pay careful attention to its reply: "Jesus I know, and Paul I know about, but who are you?" (verse 15). The evil spirit challenged them because it did not recognize them. The possessed man then leapt onto the sons and began beating them up! (verse 16). This was not a spiritual attack. This was a *physical* attack, and it looks as if the demons won. The men took off bruised and bleeding. Word spread fast about the defeat of these fallen leaders. Great fear seized the Jews and Greeks living in Ephesus, and the Lord Jesus's name was held in high honor (verses 17-20).

Note: Just because people in your prayer group, or your pastor, casts out demons, it doesn't mean you are qualified to jump right into the fight too! I cannot stress enough how dangerous it will be for you if your faith and experience is atrophied, meaning it's not exercised and is weak, because you might be taken out! These demons didn't just hear of Paul, they knew him. Demons recognized authority (or the lack thereof) in a believer's life. Does Satan *know* who you are? The Word of God is alive, and spiritual warfare is not a game. Hebrews 4 tells us that the Word of God is "living and powerful, and sharper than any two-edged sword" (verse 12). God's Word is a weapon in the hands of every blood-bought believer! But we need training in order to wield it properly. In the natural realm, if someone thought it was cool to handle a firearm with no training, no permit, no anything, he could not only hurt himself but others.

When we moved to Tennessee my husband and I entered an armory to look into acquiring carry permits. I was not ashamed to ask for assistance on how to enroll in weapons courses. Although I had previously been married to a police officer, and I have family in SWAT, this does not make me an expert at knowing how to handle a gun. Even though I've been surrounded by various weapons, I understood that if I handled a gun, it wouldn't be safe for me or anyone else. No commander in the armed forces would send their soldiers out unarmed and unprepared and certainly not without specialized training! Every soldier knows his post and submits to the direct orders of his commander. Just because one soldier's father was a general at some point, it doesn't automatically grant the son the same position. The position must be earned.

The spiritual realm and all the weapons of warfare available to us believers are no different. But church leaders are guilty every day of sending their "squad" forth as if they've been properly trained to take on the enemy. They are not submitted under leadership or any type of discipleship program but think they can go into enemy territory with the name of Jesus and slaughter all their enemies. It's not only *who* you know but *what* you know! Would you want to march into battle with a pocket knife, when your commanding officer would love nothing more than to issue you a weapon of mass destruction that is powerful enough to take out legions at one time? Leaders are telling people from the pulpit that they have authority over every demon, and then these people are engaging in warfare and being wiped out! There is a lack of balanced teaching, and God's people are literally getting beat up by the devil. The world can easily see this, so why can't we?

Necessary protocol must be in place in order to protect us from evil: authority and submission. Our authority comes first through being known by Jesus, as we are in submission to His Holy Spirit.

Second, we must be baptized with supernatural power and gifts that are available to us if we are to be victorious in spiritual warfare. The gifts aren't necessary for salvation, but are needed *weapons to combat evil.* Unfortunately, many believers have been beat up and captured by the enemy, bound by the very spirits they engaged. POWs (prisoners of war) are everywhere in the body of Christ today! We don't want our faith to weaken and atrophy! Just as order is established in the military, we, too, must submit ourselves to leadership that will train, teach, and watch over us. Let's prepare ourselves for battle like the apostle Paul and his followers who were filled with the Word and His Spirit—always ready to *exercise* and *exorcise*! Otherwise we may find ourselves engaged in a wrestling match we aren't expecting!

A CALL TO ACTION

- Are you currently in a place you don't feel you were called to because it was handed to you or expected of you?
- Are you in prayer groups because you were invited or prompted by Holy Spirit?
- Are there areas in your life where you feel overwhelmed, overpowered, or overtaken? Which areas?
- List steps you can take to reposition yourself to safety.

DAY 9

RAISE THE ROOF: DO YOU HAVE WHAT IT TAKES TO BREAK THROUGH

They uncovered the roof where [Jesus] was. So, when they had broken through, they let down the bed on which the paralytic was lying.

— Mark 2:4 NKJV

As I stood waiting on the platform of a church in the Democratic Republic of the Congo, Africa, I was moved by the massive crowd of desperate people who simply wanted to "see" Jesus. These precious people knew if they could experience a wave of His power they would be healed. In third world countries there is a hunger and thirst for more than food that nourishes the body; there is an unrelenting appetite for the power of God. This spiritual hunger drives people to travel for miles and miles through sun-scorched land with babies on their backs and broken sandals, or none at all, to attend a crusade. One particular night is forever etched in my memory, and faces are indelibly impressed upon my heart, reminding me of today's scripture reading.

The local Baptist church couldn't seat the huge number who came to this crusade, so the people were content to stand in the entrance. As I stood looking out at the crowd, I saw that some were on other's backs, straining to see all the way to the platform, while others were sitting in the open windows that surrounded the building. I will never forget the immense responsibility I felt to bring a word of hope and encouragement, followed by signs and wonders that would change their lives forever. I identified with what the apostle Paul meant when he said, "My message and my preaching were not with wise and persuasive words, but with a demonstration of the Spirit's power" (1 Corinthians 2:4). By whatever means necessary, these hungry Congolese people were not going to miss a visitation of God's healing power, especially after having endured the devastation of the brutal 100-day war that ravaged the country in 1994 and left more than 800,000 people slaughtered. In neighboring Rwanda, approximately 85 percent of Rwandans are from the Hutus tribe; the Hutus eventually overthrew the minority Tutsi tribe who dominated the country at that time.[1]

You can imagine the raw emotion I sensed, having come all the way from the United States to minister through International Relief by day and preach the gospel in crusades in the evening. Because of Hutus/Tutsi war, I fully understood the great need for spiritual and physical healing, and I felt the weight of the responsibility.

The Spirit of God moved mightily every night, but one night was special. I had spotted a particular woman in the middle of the crowd; the detailed lines of grief and shame were evident upon her face. In the midst of hundreds, I spoke boldly that this woman had been shamed in the community because she was barren and unable to carry a child. The Holy Spirit revealed that she would be pregnant by this time next year. After about five hours of preaching, I had made my way to the back room of the church to catch my breath when an elder approached me and said the woman was requesting to see me. I agreed, and she approached, falling at my feet wailing in tears. I lifted her quickly from the floor and held this weeping woman in my arms. My interpreter explained that she was hesitant to accept a local man's marriage proposal because she couldn't bear children. But that night her desire to receive a miracle from God superseded her fear of those who scorned her. Hope filled her heart as I prophesied to her that by this time next year she would conceive a son. I was informed later through correspondence with my interpreter, that this same woman married and gave birth to her baby boy a year later.

Was it easy for this woman to get to me? She had to push through the very crowds of people who knew of her and her barrenness. She broke through the crowd of rejection to claim her miracle. I felt as if I had met Hannah, the same woman who cried silently before her husband Elkanah because she couldn't bear children (1 Samuel 1). I don't know the woman's name or how she is this many years later, but I pray for her, as I do for all my African brothers and sisters I miss so dearly. After that trip, I wondered often if God would lead me back to Africa. Then, one day, a man came to fix my pool. When he handed me the bill, to my surprise, he also delivered a prophetic word. He said it would no longer be the poor countries but my own that would need what God has given me. He spoke that it was time to deliver a word to the United States. To this day, the man who fixed my pool Pastor Jason Welsh, in Southern California, is one of our dearest African American friends. Brian also chose him to be the best man at our wedding!

Again, as I reflect on Africa, I can picture vividly what it took for the paralytic in our verse today to get his breakthrough. The reality was he couldn't exercise any more of his will because he was completely paralyzed! Thank God for good friends, because it took four men to "raise the roof" for his breakthrough!

Now Jesus had entered Capernaum (Mark 2:1), and it is my assumption he went to teach at Peter's house. Verse 2 tells us so many people gathered that there was no room for any more. So the friends had to figure out another way to get their buddy to Jesus. What did these men do? They literally tore the roof off the house and lowered their friend down to Jesus's feet! (verses 3-4). I'm telling you, these men had to be the Navy Seals of their day, because it took some dedication and muscle to tear off the roof of a house and strategically lower a man down.

Scripture doesn't indicate how much this man weighed or how

tall he was, but he would have been 100 percent dead weight and unable to be of any assistance. His friends not only had to lay him on a stretcher and carry him to Peter's home (we have no idea how far they had to travel), but upon arrival, unfortunately, they discovered this house was filled to capacity. Most friends would turn around and take their unlucky friend back home. Not these warriors! These men were obviously physically, mentally, and strategically prepared for the mission, because step one was hoisting their stretcher-bound friend up the side of the house, hoping he didn't fall off! Imagine what they must've been thinking once they got him to the top of the roof—*now what do we do?* Step two, of course, was just ripping the roof from the house and lowering him down! Easy peasy, right?

Imagine yourself at a nice home Bible study when you hear noise above your head and look up to see the roof being dismantled, with four guys lowering a man on a stretcher into the living room! I can imagine all the type A personalities at this meeting—who tend to be more aggressive, time urgent, and orderly—thinking, "I sure hope Brother Pete has homeowner's insurance!" But what was our Lord's response? "Seeing their faith Jesus said to the paralyzed man, "Son, your sins are forgiven" (verse 5).

Over the years I've heard many sermons on this passage, but I have never heard the perspective I'm about to share. Yes, I see great faith displayed in the passage; but even more I recognize four amazing warriors who must have been in elite shape to execute raising a roof for this man's breakthrough! The Bible doesn't say if any of these friends were female, but why not? When I was in the Congo, a rebel uprising broke out, and it took every ounce of strength, muscle, and strategic planning I had to get past the armed rebels on the road and to a safe house. I've had to carry heavy equipment, people, and supplies at the drop of a hat! What if your breakthrough requires some heavy lifting and the only way a breakthrough can happen is by executing some type of covert operation like the one in Mark 2? I can't imagine why anyone would minimize the need for Christians to be healthy and in shape, especially when we read passages such as this one. Just as these men broke through the roof so their friend could have his breakthrough, who knows but that you may have the same honor for one of your friends. Would you be willing to go to any lengths to bring healing to someone who is unable to obtain it on their own? Remember, this paralyzed man was dead weight to his friends. He couldn't offer any physical assistance to them. So many in this very hour are paralyzed, either spiritually or physically, and are in great need for warriors to come to their rescue and do whatever it takes to save them. Are you willing to be this type of friend, even if they can offer you nothing? God always sends help to us, and the people you may be feeling jealous toward could be the very ones to raise the roof on your behalf.

A CALL TO ACTION

- Are you in need of a supernatural miracle? If so, list that need.
- Are you avoiding someone due to jealousy, pride, or any other reason, who may be able to help?
- Are there warriors around you who can offer assistance?
- Are you the one who can physically rescue someone in need? How can you go about helping that person today?

DAY 10

FINALLY OUT! HOW TO BEAT ADDICTION

Although the Lord gives you the bread of adversity and the water of affliction, your teachers will be hidden no more; with your own eyes you will see them. (Isaiah 30:20)

— Isaiah 30:20

When I was raising my two daughters, one of my best friends used to tell me she prayed her children would experience immediate consequences for their sin. I can recall at the time thinking that was quite a brutal way to pray for your children. But one day she told me her daughter was instructed clearly not to get on a moped but chose to do so anyway against her mother's better judgment. The girl drove around the neighborhood street corner and promptly crashed. Thank God she was not injured, but you had better believe she understood there would be consequences for all of her actions outside of obedience. We must grasp that direct disobedience to God's instruction can result in catastrophe. Whether immediate or delayed, there will be a result. But what about decisions that have been born from the best of intentions but were not the best choices in the long run? This is where our scripture passage for today comes to light because, while God does not afflict us, decisions *we* make can bring about times of intense affliction that eventually become our teachers.

I cannot recall making a conscious decision to take pain medication for herniated discs in my back, but I can tell you when I decided to rebel. While in high school I made choices to experiment with what are now called "gateway drugs." My mother was a cigarette smoker, so I sneaked cigarettes from the ashtray when at all possible. That led to smoking pot, which quickly escalated to cocaine. The abuse and spiritual warfare was so severe in my home that it was only a matter of time before addiction would take me captive. Honestly, I have never understood why parents bring alcohol or cigarettes in the home but instruct the children never to touch them: "Do as I say, not as do!" This behavior is so hypocritical. But even more than that, the demonic strongholds parents welcome into their homes can be catastrophic. We are at war; what we seemingly "got away with" in the past will not work in the times we are in now. For example, many preachers are declaring that drinking alcohol is not godly, and this subject is causing a war within the body of Christ. Also, there is a stigma attached to believers that leaves them fearful of being judged if they are taking medications, so they don't reach out for help. These issues are dividing believers, but I see right through the "smoke" screen. The focus shouldn't be whether you are sinning if you choose to drink or take prescriptions, but rather, will the choices you're making impair your judgment? Will your discernment still be on point when you're under the influence of these sedatives, which means "tending to calm, moderate, or tranquilize nervousness'?[1]

As a parent, I did my best to teach my daughters to discern for themselves what could possibly be detrimental to their spiritual walk. I tried to not tell them what they should do or should not do; rather, I encouraged them to discern for themselves so their choices would be their own and not entirely mine. We must ask ourselves first if our decisions will impair our discernment. If the answer is yes, are we willing to allow that sedation for an hour, a few days, or even ten years? This is not a salvation issue, but an individual's choice to be or not to be "on point" and to what degree. As for me and my house, I know as soon as I let my guard down, the enemy takes advantage. I want to say to every parent reading this: Please understand the power these choices you're making has on your home. This is not a religious issue but a choice we are all free to make. The times in which we are living do not promote purity and obedience but the contrary. Our homes should be a safety zone, not a war zone.

At some point I was introduced to Vicodin (hydrocodone) for my back pain. Everyone on my mother's side, the Gigliotti family, had undergone back surgery. All of the sexual abuse and prescription drug abuse originated on my mother's side! Trust me when I say these two abuses, more often than not, work in tandem. I had prayed for years to be set free from the back issues that caused me such great sciatic pain. I finally realized I was not going to be healed so I had better figure out how to live on this medication without it becoming a problem. This would be a good place to interject one of my famous quotes, "How's that been working for ya?" That is how the devil lies to us. Because God wasn't healing me, I would have to learn to live with extreme pain.

I had a choice to make at that point. I had exhausted every avenue. I stayed accountable to pastors, friends, and everyone I felt I could trust to help me. (Sadly, I experienced backlash from some of those I trusted). I literally begged God and searched out people with wisdom in the church to help me wean, but to no avail. One day I was in prayer and heard these words within my heart: "Gina, I will not bring your husband to you until you are off this medication. The warfare you two will experience will be off the charts. It will not come from within the members of your body but from the outside pressures of ministry. He will not be involved in this portion of your deliverance." I understood at this point I was being given the free choice to either stay on the pills for my pain or to be free from pills and live with pain. What I am going to share now is for anyone who is truly suffering from choices you've made, but you're now ready to be free, whatever the cost!

I endured the eight-month weaning process with Suboxone,

which is still a narcotic but is used for those addicted to opioids. The first night when all narcotics were out of my system, I experienced insomnia. I thought to myself, "Surely the Lord will help me to sleep since I was obedient to get off this junk." However, this was not to be the case. Because I was not healed instantly, my teachers, not one, but many, were before me. I now had to face areas of my wounded soul I had never been aware of due to being medicated. I understood what I was about to go through for the next eight months would be for the purpose of releasing the "breaker anointing" in the future! I had been delivered miraculously from three cocaine overdoses before I was twenty-one years old, but this time I knew I was about to walk this one out. You cannot take down an enemy you have never wrestled. In the sport of grappling, we learn the art of submissions—forcing our enemy to submit to us, not the other way around.

With God as my witness, I didn't sleep for eight months. The host of angel armies had their work cut out for them because there were many nights I would pass out from sheer exhaustion only to "wake up" to see I had been on the floor only about a minute or two. I could have injured myself severely. My pastor, Dr. Harold Dewberry, who has gone to be with the Lord, was up praying for me night after night. My faithful pastor was always available, mostly within the hours of 3 a.m. to 6 a.m., to take my frantic call! I can recall his sharing with me that he had a vision of an eight-armed octopus chasing me through the entire house. He said he literally thought he would die during this intense intercession. I knew no one could physically get me out of this, so I fought through with everything I had within me.

My daughter had flown in from New York for her school break, and I went running with her in Dana Point. She had no idea I was in the midst of detoxing, but I would not miss my beach run with my girl! She stayed consistently five minutes ahead that day, when normally we ran side by side. I didn't give up though, and I pushed through. I knew God had given me an innate ability to fight. This day something happened to me. I was fighting for my life, for my girls, for the nations. This run had to happen! I was fully aware I opened this door through my own choices, and now it was my war to fight.

I saw my doctor only once during this time. He made it clear I had to get some sleep, so he prescribed Ambien. I took one pill and felt my brain "zap" within twenty minutes. Brain zaps are uncontrollable electrical sensations that can occur as a result of withdrawing from antidepressants and psychotropic medications. This is all related to the serotonin in the brain. Obviously, these medications throw off all our natural levels. I was so frightened by this, I threw the bottle out and declared to the Lord I would do this medication-free, and I did! (More than nine million Americans are taking a sleep aid.)

One glorious night, I found myself walking toward the restroom in a complete stupor, uttering the words, "I'm finally out, I'm finally out, I'm finally out!" As I came to my senses, I realized I was dreaming, which meant I slept for the first time! In the dream I was running through a maze of snipers, who were positioned all around the tops of buildings, attempted to take me out. I ran out of the maze speaking those words. It was over! This war was over, and the Holy Spirit told me those I would help would not have to suffer through what I did in order to be free. Their healing would be instant. This has been true thus far!

I understand this is not your average devotional, but I refuse to follow any patterns. Addiction may be an epidemic, but this warrior has been set free! I do not "abstain," and I am not a recovering addict. I am delivered! (I will explain further in Day 22.)

Helping people to break stereotypes and patterns is what I do. I am not here to tell anyone to stop taking medication or throw out the alcohol. What I am attempting to convey is that every action we take has consequences. The first time I took prescriptions, I had no idea that it would lead to the hell I went through. Transparency will set you free. Are you willing?

*See Appendix A for more info on Zija *Moringa oleifera* and Zija XM-PM for sleep.

A CALL TO ACTION

- Have you been given specific instructions but are choosing not to listen?

- How has this disobedience affected you or your family?

- In what areas do you or family members need healing from a serious issue?

- Other than prayer, list steps you can actively take towards your miracle.

DAY 11

HOW TO RECOGNIZE WARRIORS WHO WILL FIGHT WITH YOU

These are the names of David's mighty warriors.

— 2 Samuel 23:8

The last words of David, God's mighty warrior, are written in 2 Samuel 23. I don't know about you, but I thoroughly enjoy sitting at the feet of men and women who are seasoned with God's wisdom. Generally, our society has a bad tendency to disrespect and marginalize our senior citizens, but I know better than to do that. They are brimming with rich life experiences that we can either glean from or choose to ignore. Recently, I was sitting outside a coffee shop, ready to tune everyone out and relax, when an older gentleman approached me. You know that look: they are lonely and looking for someone to talk to. As I listened, he shared snippets of his life that were filled with selfless service to our country. He recounted his fighter-jet days and incredible acts of heroism that included saving the life of his fellow fighter. This precious man needed someone to listen, and because I took the time for him, I was the one who was blessed! I then asked him, "Who is going to save you?" I had the opportunity to share Jesus with him, and this mighty warrior, who was late in life, bowed his head to accept salvation and receive eternal life. He will receive a Purple Heart in heaven!

When I read the heading at the beginning of 2 Samuel, "David's Last Words," I understand it is a moment to pause and listen to what one of God's amazing warriors had to say in his final days. The first seven verses declare his praise for God that his enemies have been cast aside and his house stands right with God. However, I want to turn our attention to the three mighty men spoken of in the next verses. I want us to pay close attention to the men who fought next to David, because, in his final words, David recognizes these men for a specific reason. We are going to break down the meanings of their names and how they apply to us and the battles we now face.

The first elite warrior was named Josheb-Basshebeth, who was the chief of the Three. Verse 8 tells us he raised his spear against eight hundred men in one encounter. His name means "one that swarms or a swarmer."[1] The Hebrew root of his name means "one that returns mentally, sits and dwells spiritually, able to refrain from evil and vices."[2] There is so much wisdom about this mighty man, and his name says it all. Can you imagine one man taking out eight hundred terrorists in one encounter? These are the types of warriors that Brian and I have surrounding us.

My husband has become a great friend and confidant to a few "Josheb-Basshebeth" type men since we settled in Tennessee. In California, Brian felt so alone and couldn't seem to connect with fellow warriors who stuck close until we set foot here. The men Brian has met this past year are swarmers; and just like a bee, they can sting the enemy, shutting off his very breath.

Does that sound a bit brutal to you? Some believers still cannot conceive the fact that Brian's background in mixed martial arts was godly; but I assure you, if their daughter was snatched off the street to be used for sex-trafficking, they would seek out a fearless warrior like Josheb-Basshebeth to rescue her. And, by the way, sex-trafficking is happening in your own neighborhood and in surrounding businesses. Prostitution and sex-trafficking rings are in full operation next door to your hair salon or grocery store. Just because you don't see sex traffickers with your own eyes, doesn't mean this evil isn't going on all around you.

I want to point out the Hebrew meaning of this man's name: "one that returns, mentally sits and dwells spiritually, able to refrain from evil and vices." The definition of *vice* is "bad or immoral behavior or habits or characteristic: a moral flaw or weakness."[3]

I know I refer to my husband often, but it is because he is exactly who he claims to be. There is nothing pretentious or fake about him. When you can find a man who is free from vices, who mentally sits and dwells spiritually, you have just found one of God's elite warriors. I have never witnessed any vice controlling Brian. He is one of the most mentally sound and stable men I have met to date. Everyone who is called to the front lines needs this type of man or woman next to them. The title of our devotion indicates you will need to be able to recognize this kind of warrior.

The second elite warrior with David was Eleazar, which means "God has helped."[4] He stood next to David when the Philistines taunted and poked fun at David. When the Philistines drew up for battle, Israel retreated. Eleazar stood his ground and killed Philistines right and left until he was exhausted, but he never let go of his sword! His hand was "stuck to the sword" (verses 9-10).

Any of us who has gone through trials that have almost taken us out understands the importance of having an Eleazar beside us. Visionaries step out and do what others never will. Noah spent years building an ark and was mocked because no one had ever seen any rainfall! You may not be able to see what is up ahead, but God does, and He is sending help.

We cannot do this life alone, and it's foolish to think we can. Everyone needs someone who will stick with them when family, friends, and the world taunt, mock or desert you. This type of harassment can wear anyone out; but when you have an Eleazar by your side, nothing will stop you! Those you thought you could trust may turn tail and run when the going gets tough and public opinion is not in your favor, but just like Eleazar did, this mighty person will chase down your naysayers. He or she will hold up your weary arms regardless of the conditions you face. This person can be recognized easily, because he or she has come to help you. I, personally, have a few women who are "Eleazars" to me. I honor and thank you!

The third elite warrior was named Shammah, which means "God is there."[5] The Philistines had mustered for battle at Lehi, in a field of lentils. Shammah stood his ground in the center of the field, successfully defending the land while routing the Philistines (verses 11-12). God is going to send someone who knows how to stand his ground upon the land, and you shall soon have victory!

We really need only three types of people, not thousands! One must be incredibly focused mentally with an innate courage to take out all opposing forces. Nothing can distract those people, not even their own thoughts. Fear and distractions are ignored. Every vice and bad habit have been left behind and they are always on point. Another will remain by your side during times you are exhausted. Every warrior needs rest after a victorious battle, and Elijah is a perfect example. He should not have been left alone after his victory because he was tired and susceptible to Jezebel. He needed an Eleazar to hold him up! You will recognize the Shammahs because they are praying for your children, land, and all things that can be taken from you during your battle. They will stand their ground and claim territory on your behalf. The fact that Shammah was in a field of lentils is prophetic in itself. May I remind you it was lentil stew that tempted Esau to give his birthright to his brother!

I prophesy your days of mourning are drawing to a close. God is sending help in this hour to deliver you from the trauma you have suffered from every battle you've fought, every addiction, and every loss. You will recover all the land and territory taken from you. Your children will return to you in their right minds, filled with truth and the power of the Holy Spirit! The time has come where you will recognize the elite warriors assigned to you. Help is on the way! Where the enemy has shut your mouth, God will cause you to trust again and ask for help. The enemy intends for you to remain mute, isolated, and alone, but God has another plan! You're about to be joined by warriors!

A CALL TO ACTION

- List the names of family members, friends, or coworkers who are in your close circle.
- Take an inventory of the character of these people and list how they've helped or hindered.
- List those who are a hindrance in your life and steps you can take to set up boundaries.
- What steps can you take to begin to surround yourself with elite warriors? Are you willing to stand alone until they arrive, or are you filling your calendar because you are afraid to be alone?

DAY 12

STAY OR SHOULD WE GO? LEPROSY IN THE CHURCH

If we say, 'We will enter the city,' the famine is in the city, and we shall die there. And if we sit here, we die also.

— 2 Kings 7:4 NKJV

Making a decision to exercise, for some, seems to be a do-or-die situation. I cannot begin to tell you how, time and time again, through the years, simply bringing up the subject of exercise makes some people step back twenty paces. I've trained clients who have made the commitment to exercise and are working their programs, but when they encourage their spouse to join in it is as if the spouse has been asked to lay down his or her life! Why do we struggle so intensely with physical discipline? I believe the answer is simple: it will cost us something. The cost varies for each of us, from losing television time to watching our favorite program on the DVR or getting some extra sleep after a hard day of work. Maybe you feel you are not physically capable so it's too late for you.

When I was the associate pastor of a church, I was preparing to deliver a message to the Sunday congregation. As I was reading the passage above in 2 Kings, I heard the Spirit of God speak to me that the church today carries a "leprous" attitude in many ways. I absolutely love when the Lord references physical challenges in the natural and draws parallels as to how we are allowing them to affect us spiritually. Let's examine today's passage and determine if perhaps we are stuck in the same place mentally where these four leprous men found themselves.

In 2 Kings 6 the prophet Elisha had prophesied that Samaria was about to face a great famine overnight. The king of Syria gathered his army and besieged Samaria, resulting in a great famine. The outcome was so horrific that a donkey's head sold for eighty shekels of silver. Let's also mention dove droppings were for sale (verses 24-25). Dear Lord Jesus, if that isn't a famine, I don't know what is! One day as the king of Israel was passing by a wall he heard a woman crying out for help. She had been in discussion with another woman, and they had agreed they would boil and eat their two sons, one on the first day and the other woman's son the next day. But the second woman hid her son instead. So the distraught woman approached the king for help (verses 26-29). Imagine the desperation in Israel.

Now enter four lepers sitting at the entrance of the gate (7:3). They began to discuss their options, knowing that if they got up from their position and entered into Samaria, they would die of hunger. They also determined among themselves if they didn't move but chose to remain where they were, death was going to be their outcome as well. These men were faced with a decision, knowing their lives were at stake either way. After discussing what seemed to be their only two options, they decided to take a crazy risk and surrender to the army of the Syrians hoping against hope their lives might be spared (verse 4). I absolutely love what takes place next because I can hear in my spirit the word, "*Surprise*!" At dusk the lepers headed over to the Syrian camp. But when they came to the edge of the camp, not a man was to be found (verse 5).

That's not what you expected was it? The prophet Elisha had already prophesied what was coming regarding the famine, and then the Lord caused the Syrian army to hear the noise of chariots, horses, and a great army advancing towards them! This sound was so loud that they assumed the king of Israel had hired both the Hittites and Egyptians to attack them! So the Syrians fled in terror, abandoning all their food and treasures. The lepers could not believe their eyes! They went tent by tent, gathering up silver, gold, and clothing. Each of these men hid the plunder and then went back for more (verses 6-8). My God, what a word of hope for all of us who feel stuck!

The fact that these men were lepers should speak volumes of hope to our hearts. When we grasp the revelation of how this passage and their disease relates to the church today, we can then apply the underlying wisdom and be set free. These are not merely Bible stories for us to read for entertainment but to understand God sent His Word to heal our disease and deliver us from our own self-destruction (Psalm 107:20).

Leprosy is a chronic infection caused by the bacteria *Mycobacterium lepromatosis*. Initially this infection displays no symptoms and can stay this way from five to twenty years! Symptoms that develop include (listen closely) granulomas of the *nerves, respiratory tract, skin*, and *eyes*, even resulting in the *lack of ability to feel pain* from injuries resulting from infection.

God does not curse us nor destroy us; we do it to ourselves. When we walk in obedience the natural fruits will be blessings on all sides. *Disobedience simply results in curses*. We create atmospheres conducive to cultivating blessings or curses. No one can ever say we serve a mean Father. His Word is filled with step-by-step instructions to teach us how to walk in health, wealth, and blessing. Leviticus 13 spells out clearly the law concerning how to deal with leprosy. For all those with religious spirits, keep in mind the Old and New Testaments are both relevant; one does not replace the other. In Matthew 5:17-20 Jesus said:

> Do not think that I have come to abolish the Law or the Prophets; I have not come to abolish them but to fulfill them. For truly I tell you, until heaven and earth disappear, not the smallest letter, not

> the least stroke of a pen, will by any means disappear from the Law until everything is accomplished. Therefore anyone who sets aside one of the least of these commands and teaches others accordingly will be called least in the kingdom of heaven, but whoever practices and teaches these commands will be called great in the kingdom of heaven. For I tell you that unless your righteousness surpasses that of the Pharisees and the teachers of the law, you will certainly not enter the kingdom of heaven.

We are instructed not to set aside these teachings or we will be called the least in the Kingdom. Jesus came to this earth to fulfill the law.

Now back to leprosy. The Lord spoke to His friend Moses and explained that if the skin of the body was swollen, scabbed, or had a bright spot on it, the person must be brought to Aaron the priest or one of his sons who were also priests. It was then the priest's responsibility to examine this sore. He was given specifics concerning how to identify the condition in order to determine if the man was infectious or "unclean." If the priest concluded that the sore could be infectious to others, he was instructed by God to isolate this person. On the seventh day the sore would be examined again to be sure it had not spread. If the sore was unchanged the leprous person was to be isolated for another seven days. This process of seven occurred three times. Upon the final examination the priest was to determine if the sore was a scab. If it was scabbed over, and had not spread any further, then it certainly would not spread to another! Lastly, the leprous person was to wash his clothes and he would be considered clean (Leviticus 13:1- 46).

I know God is cleaning house and will no longer allow the conditions of spiritual leprosy to spread throughout His body. All may "appear" well, but just like this disease, spiritual leprosy can lie dormant for years. However, when the symptoms present themselves, we have a people unable to feel pain due to repeated injuries and religious abuse! Infection is beneath the surface, but it's about to be made known so the leper may be healed. The times are now demanding the priests or pastors of their flock care for those who have been severely wounded. The instruction has already been given throughout this passage, and we must not only contain the lepers for the good of the entire body but for the lepers' own healing and deliverance. (Hence this is why it's vital that traumatized leaders take a sabbatical in order to be healed, or they spread leprosy).

Sanctification and purification must return to the body of Christ or we will continue to see many believers stuck at the gate and unable to enter into their destinies filled with healing and blessing. It's time all of us take a chance and step out past those things that hinder our own minds and cause us great anxiety and infection. We are *not* called to be a church of lepers but of *leapers*. Are we willing to take a *leap* of faith, remembering we serve a God of miracles who is more than capable of confusing the enemy who has been causing us fear and anxiety? The very enemy that we think is waiting for us beyond the gates has already been sent on another assignment. To your surprise, blessing in all areas awaits you, and your sores will no longer limit you. Just as the lepers plundered silver, they also plundered new clothes, which are a symbol of new mantles! They were made clean as they moved from where they were. All of us are positioned outside of something, but we can choose whether or not we stay and die or take a risk, get up, and go! The enemy wants you to remain an outcast, but you will experience healing within the movement of your active faith!

A CALL TO ACTION

- List any areas where you feel stuck physically or spiritually.
- What fears are keeping you stuck outside the gate?
- List any physical or emotional places you know you are covering up.
- What action steps can you take to move forward in these areas?

DAY 13

UNDER THE INFLUENCE: SEDUCED BY A WORD

> **"I too am a prophet, as you are. And an angel said to me by the word of the LORD: 'Bring him back with you to your house.'" (1 Kings 13:18)**
>
> — 1 KINGS 13:18

Charismatic leaders can be quite intoxicating. They have the right style, personality, and risky faith that draw many unsuspecting people into their web. A pastor, for whom I hold great respect, told me once that many prophets are "mentally ill" as they operate in their prophetic gifting! I agree wholeheartedly. In my experience many of them can't hold a normal conversation without flaunting their entire charismatic biblical lingo. Attempting mature communication with them is like pulling teeth. These conversations leave my head spinning but not my spirit stirring. So keep your spiritual eyes open, because these prophets will come into your sphere of influence, if they haven't already. There's no mistaking that if you don't have a handle on your purpose, and are not able to identify their motives, their influence can destroy your destiny. Many of us who have gone through the fire, and have been tested in various forms, may be quick to say we would have no problem identifying someone under the influence of a lying spirit. Within the fire of affliction we have learned to not give into seducing or lying spirits. Nonetheless, there is an ungodly influence sweeping the body of Christ off its feet and away from its destiny.

In 1 Kings 13 we read about an unnamed prophet who was sent to King Jeroboam (verse 1). But just because we don't know his name, it doesn't mean he was not a mover and a shaker. He prophesied that the human bones of those the king was sacrificing to idols would fall upon him. This king was so infuriated at the prophet that he reached out to grab him, but his own arm suddenly became paralyzed and shriveled up. He couldn't pull back the very finger he pointed at the man of God (verses 2-4). This type of miracle would cause any of your haters to repent and ask for forgiveness. At Jeroboam's request, the prophet prayed for his healing and Jeroboam's shriveled hand was restored. The king immediately invited the man of God to his palace, but he refused, stating in no uncertain terms that he couldn't be bought. There was nothing materialistic he could be offered that would cause him to defy God's orders to go back the way he came. He was instructed by God to not eat bread or drink water and to take a different road (verses 6-10).

After a victory such as this one, we can imagine what this man was feeling as he continued on his journey: *Thank God for your awesome display of power! You really showed them what's up at the altar; and if that wasn't enough, you stretched out your hand to my hater*. That would have been a great day of ministry for any prophet.

Anytime an up-and-coming leader is brought to the forefront or in the limelight, there will always be an "old prophet" who hears about you. The story in 1 Kings 13 goes on to say this old prophet who was living in Bethel heard about what took place. He told his sons to mount up the donkeys because he was going after the man. Once he found the man of God, he invited him to go back and eat with him at his home. The man of God, who was minding his own business resting under an oak tree, began to tell this old prophet that he could not. He explained his strict instructions from God and that he could not go back the way he just came (verses 11-17). The old prophet then said, "I too am a prophet, as you are. And an angel said to me . . . bring him back" (verse 18). So the man of God returned to eat and drink with him at his house. Even though this old prophet was under the influence of a lying spirit, the gifts and call of God are irrevocable (verses 18b-19; Romans 11:29). He began prophesying from God that the man of God had defied God's instructions. The old prophet spelled out exactly what the man of God did wrong and then told him his body would not be buried in the tomb of his ancestors (verses 20-22). After this wonderful dinner meeting filled with excitement and prophecy, the old prophet saddled up the donkey and sent the man of God off to his death. He was mauled by a lion as he traveled (verses 23-24).

We have to be discerning now and in the future because tares have been sown among the wheat. They speak like us and prophesy like us, but they are under the influence of a lying spirit as well as other spirits. This precious man of God from the scripture passage was obviously committed to God and boldly prophesied what many on platforms nowadays wouldn't dare to say, knowing they run the risk of never being invited back for the next conference or telethon. And they definitely would not have won the Prophet of the Year award, as they attempted to clean up the church house with words such as the ones the man of God delivered. But he was faithful! What's concerning about the story in 1 Kings 13 is that the prophet appeared to do everything right! He obeyed God's commands and prophesied against the king, knowing he would be arrested and thrown in jail if God did not send a miraculous sign that He was with him. The man of God had a forgiving heart. This prophet rejected the money that accompanied going back home with the king. How many of us, after a great victory, would simply go home or out to dinner after a meeting? The decision seems simple, right? No! We have to be so in tune with the Spirit of God in these last days. Lives depend on it.

Again, the man of God was not influenced by the money offered by Jeroboam, so what did he miss with this old prophet? I am going to read between the lines on this one! He needed a word and he got it!

The old prophet first identified himself as a prophet just like him. I don't know about you, but when I meet someone, I don't need the person to tell me whether he or she is a prophet. Doesn't the Bible tell us, "The spirits of the prophets are subject to the prophets?" (1 Corinthians 14:32 NKJV).

The Greek word for spirits is *pneuma*, meaning their heart, breath, mind, or wind. We get the medical term *pneumonia* from this root word. When people have pneumonia they have an inflammatory condition of the lungs. They can't breathe! Their lungs are restricted from taking in air! As soon as this man of God was told the old man was also a prophet, and had a word from God, it was over! All the victory and boldness the man of God displayed, the future of many he could have influenced, came to end, because someone under the influence gave him a word. He was not only taken off the path he was on, but his destiny was destroyed. The man of God was sitting under an oak tree, likely being refreshed and thinking about the amazing victories he was privileged to be a part of. Persons who are washed up in their own purposes will seek out those who are in the midst of theirs. They will come and tell you how everything should be done and boast about all the works they accomplished by their own hands. Beware of those who are eager to tell you all about themselves.

Here is the nugget of gold in all of this wisdom. What I am about to share I learned through being submitted to others in leadership. Through submission to reliable authority and remaining in position I learned this valuable nugget of discernment. Anytime you tell someone God spoke to you and that person turns and tells you God told him or her something different for you, pay attention! As I mentor and counsel people, I may be given specific instructions for them first with regard to the issue at hand. As the man of God told the old prophet, "God told me not to go back." But the old prophet replied, "Well, God told me you are to come back." Hold up! Mature, spirit-led prophets will never tell you something contrary to what God already spoke to you. Even if what you heard is wrong, a mature, under-the- influence-of-the-Holy Spirit-leader will pray for you and wait for you to return. It's sorcery to attempt to control another person with "a word from the Lord."

Here's how the encounter between the man of God and the old prophet should have gone down: The man of God says, "God told me not to return, but thank you for the invitation." The old prophet responds, "Please obey as you feel God is speaking to you. If you change your mind, you are welcome at my home."

Before President Trump was elected, I heard the Lord say, "From the White House to the Courthouse to the church house, I AM cleaning house." I've had pastors tell me, "God loves His church and we need to be kind." I agree. However, let's be the "kind" of leaders who expose lying spirits that have taken control of our brothers and sisters in the church and are leading the young ones straight into the grave of unfilled destiny! Are we really foolish enough to think the first two houses are being renovated before our very eyes, but God will allow leaders in His church who are under the influence to continue with business as usual?

Though this story in 1 Kings 13 is often preached with excitement about the withering hand extended against God's anointed, I am more inclined to heed the warning of how this wonderful man of God left the earth prematurely. I certainly don't want to make the same mistakes.

Bible stories are not written for our entertainment but as a guide to how we are to navigate through war. Casualties of war are inevitable, but we do not have to be one of them. Instead of the great seduction being the love of money, do you suppose it could possibly be the desperation of a believer whose lamp is empty and in need of a word?

A CALL TO ACTION

- Can you think of people or leaders whom you judge or criticize? If so, ask God for forgiveness and pray for them.
- Has God asked you to do something specific, but you are being influenced by other people?
- Do you always feel the need to "toot your own horn" and let everyone know who you are?
- List the people and/or things that influence you. Take an inventory as to whether they are positive or negative.

DAY 14

PRINCIPLES NEVER CHANGE, BUT METHODS DO

[Jesus] spat on the ground and made clay with the saliva; and He anointed the eyes of the blind man with the clay.

— John 9:6 NKJV

"Who is ready to receive healing?" You look around and see people getting out of their seats and running toward the altar for the laying on of hands from the popular evangelist. You have suffered year after year with pain all throughout your body. Will this be the day your prayers will be answered? You have come to the end of your rope. Your reserve tank is empty, and the indicator pointing to your faith is on E as well. You are not alone, and neither was the blind man in our story.

Jesus came in contact with many sick and hurting people on a daily basis. One day He passed by a man who had been blind since birth (John 9:1). Of course this man couldn't see Jesus walking by. But I do know that people who suffer with disabilities have to learn to use other areas that are stronger. Just as it is with anyone who suffers from blindness, I can imagine this man's other four senses were in high gear. He may have heard Jesus's footsteps or felt His presence intensely drawing close or maybe the scent of the Rose of Sharon filled the blind man's nostrils. John didn't say, but he did tell us that the man's blindness was from birth, so I can imagine he learned to key in on many conversations that took place around him as the gossip of his family's "sin" caused them heartache. Even the disciples closest to Jesus asked who the big sinner in the family was. Could it be the man himself, or his parents? (verse 2). Jesus answered, "Neither this man nor his parents sinned, but that the works of God should be revealed in him" (verse 3 NKJV). Then we see Jesus do something very unusual. Jesus spit in the dirt and proceeded to make mud (verse 6). I don't know about you, but when I see a man spit in the dirt, it doesn't leave a puddle big enough to turn dirt into mud! This was no little spittle that hit the ground! Jesus had to really hunker down and give it a good one to make this mud! As if this method wasn't unusual enough, Jesus smeared the mud all over this blind man's eyes and then instructed him to go wash in the pool of Siloam (which means "sent"). To everyone's astonishment, the blind man actually obeyed Jesus and ran back to Him possessing perfect vision! (verse 7).

We know God's principles never change, but are we aware that His methods do? We know the Word of God never changes, but the *times* we live in do. So, if the times are changing, we must move with God and be willing to move His way. God's ways are not ours; but the question is, are we willing to obey whatever peculiar method He uses to heal others? In addition, are we willing to be the recipient of an unorthodox method?

It is human tendency to attempt to figure out how God is going to rescue us from our trials. As we reflect on the ways He has delivered us in the past, we naturally assume He will use the same ways. I personally have never witnessed anyone smear spit onto the eyes of a blind person, but I am completely open to whatever strange plan God may direct! I sense what John 9 is communicating through this story is the supernatural, unwavering faith in God's ability to move on our behalf, whatever the cost and whatever the method. I wonder what our response would be if this technique was used today?

Picture yourself running up to the altar for prayer; instead of an elder grabbing the anointing oil, the preacher spits into his hand, prays, and plasters it across your face! I can venture to say your first response might be "Next time I will just keep that appointment with my optometrist." However, I sense there is a deeper revelation in the passage we are supposed to grasp.

What happened after Jesus rubbed the mud on the blind man's eyes is the key. Though the man was probably confused, he still responded in immediate obedience, which resulted in 100 percent healing of his blind eyes. And Scripture tells us he came back! Who did he come back to?

I want to look at two characters in this story: the neighbors and the Pharisees. When the blind man returned to those who were familiar with him, he was so unrecognizable that they weren't even sure they were seeing the same person. They needed more details such as how something this unbelievable could happen and who was responsible (verses 8-12). The formerly blind man answered his neighbors' questions, but the methods he described didn't fit their presuppositions. These people needed to determine if the man's healing really was from God; so, instead of making up their own minds, they brought him to the Pharisees (verses 13-17). Well, it all went to hell in a hand basket from here, because these religious leaders squashed this miracle immediately! You can always find some naysayer who thoroughly enjoys discrediting your miracle or somehow explains it away. If the naysayers can't deny the healing, they will either discredit the one it came through or the way around. God chooses odd, out-of-the-box tactics in order to draw out and expose all the haters and religious spirits. They are lurking on the outskirts of your faith, just waiting for opportunities to tear you down as well as the one who sent you. At the same time, those who love you and have watched you suffer will be challenged to stand up for your miracle when they are questioned. How bold and courageous will those who have encircled you really be when questioned about the acts of Jesus concerning your life?

The story goes on to explain that his parents were questioned about this miracle. Instead of boldly declaring their own faith and acting as eyewitnesses to this miracle, they told the Pharisees to go ask their son, since he was an adult. Who will stand up in the face of religious spirits without passing the buck? You can declare God's methods are unusual, but they work!

I sincerely believe our focus isn't supposed to solely rest on the means but the outcome that resulted. God's creative styles are His own. It is our responsibility to obey what *He* requires of us—not what our pastor, best friend, or neighbors expect. True followers of Jesus Christ will live out loud in both word and deed. He is trying to move all of us to a place of radical faith that will result in utterly destroying all of our presuppositions. To presuppose is "to suppose beforehand" or "to be based on the idea that something is true or will happen."[1]

Many judgments are being twisted together that result in skewed opinions. Some would say President Trump's methods are radical, or even reckless, but if we pay close attention to the results of these actions, what we learn is undeniable. Each "method of madness" and every relentless tweet draws out the motives and intentions of everyone on both sides of the political aisle who gets involved. We see three distinct sides and opinions revealed through the president's approach: the good, bad, and indifferent. Scripturally let's take a look at three types of people: (1) people who walk in truth; (2) people who walk in lies; and (3) those who want to remain in the middle to keep from making waves. Revelation 3:21 calls the third category of people "lukewarm." "Because you are lukewarm—neither hot nor cold—I am about to spit you out of my mouth." The definition of lukewarm is "not enthusiastic: not having or showing energy or excitement" or "not very interested or eager."[2] How many believers and Christian leaders have you noticed who prefer to remain safely neutral when it comes to politics or social issues such as abortion or homosexuality? This, my friend, is the response of lukewarm Christians!

Interestingly, it was the spit of Jesus that healed this precious blind man, and it will be that same spit that will bring judgment. God's glorious Word is so full of prophetic revelation and insight! I declare, we are about to witness the most unorthodox methods being displayed by the hands of God's people who are willing to live out loud in the "on fire" category! Many people who have been living in spiritual blindness will run to the altars to receive their long-awaited healing. Then they will return 100 percent healed, unrecognizable to those who had been familiar with their suffering. This will naturally create a separation of the good, bad, and indifferent. The unorthodox ways of healing that didn't fit anyone's presumptions will result in a mass exodus of the people who judged incorrectly those who have been healed and made wrong assumptions concerning their afflictions.

Are you ready to receive your healing? Just be aware that the manner this time around may be unusual! But, just as it was for the blind man, I hear Jesus saying to you, "You did not sin, nor did your parents, but that the works of God should be revealed through you."

A CALL TO ACTION

- Do you tend to believe what you hear about others without any proof?
- Do you tend to jump to your own conclusions when someone is sick or doing things you don't agree with?
- Are you open to whatever method God may use to change your situation or theirs?
- Will you boldly admit to others how God worked in your life?

DAY 15

TURNOVERS, INTERCEPTIONS, AND FUMBLES: STOLEN IDENTITY & INCEST

You brought your people Israel in, turning it [the inhabitants of the land] over permanently to your people.

— 2 Chronicles 20:7 MSG

God has a game plan for your life, and we know the enemy would love nothing better than to destroy your identity at your very conception. However, if we can recognize the strategy of the enemy and from where his forces come, we can plan our own strategy against him. How I wish that what I am teaching you today had been explained to me in my younger years. I believe that if I had understood how to recognize and identify the demonic forces that had been assigned to make war against me and my destiny I would not have made so many mistakes.

In my early years I was fully aware that my mother had been sexually abused; but if you had told me that incest was a part of this evil, I would have been shocked. I knew molestation and pornography were in my family's history, but incest too? Oh my Lord! Thankfully, I had experienced healing from my own stolen innocence as a five-year-old little girl and the great trauma this experience caused me before my first child was conceived. The joy that flooded my soul when I held each of my children for the first time is unexplainable!

After the birth of my first daughter Ronni Marie, I was caught up in the Spirit with Jesus for more than ten minutes, apparently praying in tongues very loudly in the presence of the doctor and nurses. Jesus held Ronni in His arms and then stretched her toward me to give her back. My immediate response was "No. You hold her!" At a very young age, I had grown so close with Jesus out of desperation during unfathomable abuse, and He had brought me comfort and peace in the darkest of times. The thought of my taking her out of His hands was out of the question. Jesus gently responded by saying, "Always remember, I held her first." I was 100 percent present as the nurse handed her to me and said, "Wow, you must've really wanted her!" She spoke a prophetic truth beyond what anyone in that room could have ever known. There is nothing I wouldn't do to protect my innocent, sweet daughter.

The second double-portion blessing came fifteen months later. Labor with Lauren was very short—only three pushes. Then I was given the honor of delivering her myself! Dr. Ronlove calmly entered my room and asked me if I would like to deliver her. I was thrilled as he instructed me to bend down and grab her just under the shoulders. I pulled her directly to my chest so I was the first one to touch her!

I have made mistakes raising my daughters, as I suppose every imperfect mother has. But one fact can never be denied: I have abounding unconditional love for those two girls. Because I was unwanted by my own jealous and hateful mother, the gratitude of being entrusted with two daughters still overwhelms me to this day! And how about the name Dr. Ronlove? The girls' father's name was Ron, and he loved his daughters passionately!

Let's take a look at our scripture. In 2 Chronicles 20 we find Jehoshaphat staring down the spears of three forces that were ready to take the destiny of Israel. The Moabites, Ammonites, and the Meunites were all poised to make war against Jehoshaphat (verse 1).

Throughout Old Testament history the Moabites were a constant thorn in Israel's side. Their original ancestor was Moab, who was actually the child of Lot and his incestuous daughter (Genesis 19:37). Then we see the Ammonites first mentioned in verse 38, as Lot and his two daughters ended up in a cave, escaping God's fiery judgment from Sodom and Gomorrah. Assuming their chances for children and a future had gone up in smoke, these two desperate girls took matters into their own hands. They decided to get their father drunk and have sex with him. Lot ended up hammered and had no idea he had sexual relations with both daughters! (verses 30-38). They had just escaped the land of incest. Guess what spirit they carried into the next land? Third, the Meunites, first mentioned in 1 Chronicles 4:41, are directly connected to Moab. What a tangled web we weave!

As we take a closer look at 2 Chronicles 20 we discover that God is about to turn over these forces into Israel's hands. When I first read this chapter, and the phrase "turning it over" in verse 7, I thought immediately of football. We are going to discuss three terms from the game of football and then relate them to the three forces at war in Jehoshaphat's life and our lives as well.

The first term we discuss is a *turnover.* A turnover is when the team with the football loses possession of it and the ball is then recovered by the other team. Generally this occurs because the opposite team hits the player without warning. Has something hit you so hard that you lost possession of something dear to you? Was it your mind, dreams, marriage, or your children? I hear the Spirit of God saying, "It's turnover time. You shall possess that which was stolen." I want to state clearly that a turnover is through no fault of your own. There are times in life when we get blindsided and hit so hard that the result is years of suffering, but you're about to regain possession.

Secondly, an *interception* is when a pass is intended to be caught by a same-team player, but an opposing player catches the ball instead. Did you work very hard for something only to have it intercepted by another person? Maybe it was your spouse and adultery happened—another player took your husband or wife. Possibly you worked hard to achieve a promotion, yet a co-worker was awarded the job.

Third, a *fumble* is when a player loses control of the ball and, thus, possession of it. An example would be if a quarterback makes a perfect throw to his receiver, but for some reason the receiver drops it. Please understand fumbles have happened to all of us at times in our lives, times when we knew we totally blew it. Something or someone came our way and we dropped the ball. A fumble is an accidental loss, and there's nothing you could have done to stop it. Our families or those close to us can be perfect reminders of everything we've fumbled in our lives. We all make mistakes, but God promises to work them out for our good. It's important to forgive yourself even if those around you choose not to.

Jehoshaphat received an intelligence report about what was heading his way. He was so shaken that he cried out to God for help and ordered a nationwide fast (2 Chronicles 20:2-3). Jehoshaphat understood that it would take weapons of mass destruction to tear down these incestuous armies!

We have got to get serious about taking down the forces that have taken out our families. Again, we may have experienced turnovers, interceptions, and fumbles, but God is telling us today the same thing He told Jehoshaphat thousands of years ago. Everything you have lost, regardless of how you lost it, will be turned over, back into your full possession.

What can we learn from Lot's former homeland and the behaviors of his daughters? They were only acting out as citizens of Sodom, their birthplace! These girls grew up in a completely "tolerant" society, and obviously their father had no problem with the unabashed evils that were practiced (Genesis 13:12; 18:20; 19:1). When we are passive and tolerant toward the blatant sin going on around us, rest assured sin will find its way into our homes and the lives of our children.

Here is the definition the Holy Spirit gave to me for tolerance: *the ability or willingness to accept a particular existence of opinions or behavior that one does not necessarily agree with*. Why would we tolerate behavior that we are not in unity with? God cannot command a blessing where sin abounds. True love disciplines and changes people. *Tolerance accepts and allows evil disguised as good to prevail.* It's time for evil to be eradicated and good to prevail. Whether you've experienced turnovers, interceptions, or fumbles—or possibly all three—I want to encourage you in this season. Everything that was stolen from you will be recovered. Some people have lost their innocence due to incest, but I declare that what the enemy stole, he has to let go of now. I am living proof that what started out in my life as a playground for the enemy has transitioned into a battleground. My mission is to help many people recover the "ball" they lost and assist them to the end zone, which in football is the scoring area! God's power team is being assembled, and you're his number one draft choice. He brought His people Israel into the land, turning it over to them! It's turnover time!

A CALL TO ACTION

- Are you a victim of sexual abuse/incest?
- Have you told anyone about this? If yes, what was their response?
- Identify turnovers, interception and fumbles you've experienced.
- Seek professional help if you need to navigate through these memories.

DAY 16

HAMAN WILL HANG HIMSELF: THE LORD WILL VINDICATE HIS KINGS AND QUEENS

King Xerxes asked Queen Esther, "Who is he? Where is he—the man who has dared to do such a thing?" Esther said, "An adversary and enemy! This vile Haman!"

— Esther 7:5-6

One day, a couple of years ago, I was enjoying an intense workout at the gym when all of a sudden, I was overcome with the presence of the Lord. There are times when He speaks to us, and there are other times His presence is overwhelming. This was one of those days. I ran out of the gym to my car and broadcast a message, which to date has received thousands of views both on social media and our YouTube channel, Truth-N-Love Ministry Int'l The WARrens. The title alone, "Haman Is About to Hang Himself! The Lord Is Vindicating His Kings/Queens," captures the attention of many people who have been wounded by their adversaries but have yet to be vindicated. The message in its entirety is one of hope and redemption. I was compelled by the Lord to include portions of this teaching into this devotional. I encourage you to read all of chapters 6 and 7 in the book of Esther.

The book of Esther speaks to all of us, because deep down inside every warrior wants to be a superhero. The story of Esther's setup for royalty began one evening when King Xerxes of Persia called his lovely wife, Queen Vashti, so he could show her off in front of all his dinner guests. The Bible says she was indeed beautiful. However, Queen Vashti refused to come. We have to understand that according to their law, her actions betrayed the king. King Xerxes and his nobles were also concerned that her refusal would set a bad example for all the other wives once word got around. If the queen refused her husband, then the other women would surely follow suit. I think it's important to note that the king and his buddies were plastered on Persia's finest wine, so maybe his queen didn't want to be paraded around like common palace entertainment in front of a crowd of sloppy drunk men. This is my take on the queen's response; but, either way, it landed her in hot water. She may have kept her pride, but she lost her royal position because of this decision (Esther 1:1–2:4).

A Jew named Mordecai lived within the kingdom in the citadel of Susa. Mordecai had a young cousin, Hadassah, or Esther, whom he had taken as his own daughter after her father and mother died (2:5-7). Esther now enters the scene as one of the many young virgins gathered from every province under the king's rule to be brought into the palace harem. These young girls would undergo a year of beauty treatments and then be brought before King Xerxes as candidates for the position of queen. Mordecai had instructed Esther to not disclose her nationality and family background as a Jew. He checked constantly on her well-being and kept a close eye on his beloved Esther. She caught the attention of the man who had been put in charge of the girls as well as the attention of the king himself (verses 8-18).

Now let's begin to set up the verse for our devotional reading. As I mentioned earlier, Mordecai was always on post checking on Esther's welfare. I see this warrior not only as a protector but one who positioned himself in the right place at the right time. Mordecai was sitting at the king's gate one day when he overheard a couple of the king's own angry officials, plotting to assassinate him! He gathered this "intel" and wasted no time passing the information on to Queen Esther, who then reported it to King Xerxes, giving credit to Mordecai. Evil was exposed, and these traitors were hung on the gallows (verses 19-23).

Enter Haman, who had been appointed to a high position by King Xerxes. Mordecai refused to bow to Haman when he walked by, which infuriated Haman. Not wishing to single out Mordecai, Haman began to devise a plot to kill all the Jews (3:1-6). He told King Xerxes that there were certain people living in the land who didn't fit in their fine kingdom. Their customs and ways were different from the ways of everybody else, and worse, they disregarded the king's laws. Haman began to convince the king that these people were an affront, and the king should order that they be destroyed. Haman further told the king that he would finance this mass execution personally and deposit ten thousand talents of silver in the royal treasury to pay the men who carried out the genocide. So the king left the decision to Haman, and Haman began to execute his plan (verses 7-15).

Once again, Mordecai learned of this plot, tore his clothes and began to mourn and wail throughout the city. Esther heard that her beloved cousin Mordecai was fasting and mourning in sackcloth and ashes because Haman was plotting to annihilate their people! Mordecai sent word to Esther that the time had come to blow her cover and reveal her nationality. He told her that she must approach the king if the Jewish people were to have a chance of survival (4:1-8).

Now, every warrior will be faced with a defining moment in which he or she will have to risk everything in order to do the right thing and face evil head on, whatever the cost. Esther reminded Mordecai that the penalty for approaching the king in the inner court without being summoned could be death (verses 10-11). Mordecai sent a message back to Esther that said, "Do not think that because you are in the king's house you alone of all the Jews will escape" (verse 13). Then, in verse 14, Mordecai gives one of the best-known statements in the entire Bible: "For if you remain silent at this time, relief and deliverance for the Jews will arise from another place, but you and your father's family will perish. And who knows but that you have come to your royal position for such a time as this?"

The bond between these two is evident and is woven throughout the next events. Esther replied to Mordecai "Go and get all the Jews living in Susa together. Fast for me. Don't eat or drink for three days, either day or night. I and my maids will fast with you. If you will do this, I'll go to the king, even though it's forbidden. If I die, I die" (verses 15-16).

Obviously, the unity, prayer, and fasting of the Jews proved to be vital to the strategy that unfolded. Esther devised a wise plan, and she invited both Haman and the king to join her for a banquet (5:1-8). Wow! Imagine serving dinner to the very adversary who desires to annihilate your people, your family, and your loved ones! Preparing a meal for this man had to take wisdom and courage. The problem for Haman was, he had no idea what this warrior princess was really planning to serve up! All the while Haman was bragging to his buddies that he alone was the special guest joining the king, while at the same time having gallows built to hang Mordecai (verses 9-14).

While the evil plot thickens behind the scenes to take out Mordecai, we learn that at the same time Mordecai's name is being brought before the king. Always remember, when evil comes in like a flood, the Lord is preparing to raise up a *standard* against it. You are that standard! Mordecai was about to be honored for spoiling the previous assassination plot on the king's life. You see, what he had done years prior was about to yield public fruit! Haman, the very one who plotted Mordecai's death, was the one who had to place a beautiful robe upon him and parade him through the city streets in honor (6:1-11).

The time had come for the lavish dinner, hosted by the Jewish queen. Right in front of Haman, the king granted Esther whatever her heart desired, "even up to half the kingdom" (7:1-2). This clever woman must have heard the old saying, "The way to a man's heart is through his stomach," because she planned not only one banquet for her husband and Haman, but two! After the second scrumptious meal and fine wine, Esther had the king eating out of the palm of her hand. As he was sipping his after-dinner drink, she went right to the point: "If I have found favor with you, Your Majesty, and if it pleases you, grant me my life—this is my petition. And spare my people—this is my request. For I and my people have been sold to be destroyed, killed, and annihilated" (verses 3-4). Esther did not mention Haman, but the question came from the mouth of the king: "Who is he? Where is he—the man who has dared to do such a thing?" (verse 5). Wait for it . . . "Esther said, An adversary and enemy! This vile Haman!" (verse 6). (Remember devotional 4: "The Fire Is Kindled. Will You Follow at a Safe Distance?" Haman experienced public exposure in the presence of his friends.) Esther remained undercover only a short time before she revealed her true identity. I want to point out if it were not for Haman her true identity would have remained hidden.

Thank God for your adversaries and enemies! Praise Him for those who despise you and plot against your destiny. For at the very hour they are plotting and speaking lies into each other's ears, there are others speaking on your behalf to the Father! Jesus is reminding the Father about every evil plot you exposed, every family you helped, and those whom you served and gave of yourself in their time of need—every "Esther" you took under your wing and protected. This is the hour that both the Mortdecais and the Esthers are to be honored because two are better than one—one protected, guarded, and exposed evil; the other rose to save an entire nation. One couldn't have succeeded without the other! Just like Mordecai, your Haman will have no choice but to place a robe upon your shoulders and parade you around the city in honor. Just like Esther, the royal robe will be placed upon your shoulders, and you will have direct access to the inner courts of heaven. In this final hour, the Esthers will be privy to heaven's strategies and plans. Jesus paid the price on the cross, granting to us an all-access pass to the Father, but we must also remember what both Mordecai and Esther endured in order to save their people. Mordecai dared to expose evil plots by evil men who were on the inside! He didn't just "pray about it and wait to see how it worked out." He was stationed twice in the right place, at the right time, even though he was stationed *outside* the courtyard and not *inside*. You, too, may feel as though you've been assigned to a place outside the courtyard and away from the action, but this was the exact location where Mordecai overheard the terroristic threats. Because of that, a robe or "mantle" was placed upon his shoulders for all to see.

Esther had to muster up inner courage and face the fear of possible death. She also had to choose to be politically incorrect in order to save her people. The royal robe was placed on her shoulders, granting her authority as a queen.

Rise and shine, kings and queens of the Most High God, for Haman shall tie a noose around his own neck for all to see! The very plot that has been executed to take you out will be the very manner in which your adversaries will be taken out. The Lord will vindicate His kings and queens in this final hour!

A CALL TO ACTION

- How far back can you trace your family history on your mother's side? Father's? If you were adopted like Esther, do you know the history of your birth mother/father?

- Describe some of the challenges you have faced as a result of the way in which you were raised.

- Can you recall times in your life when you have acted as a Mordecai, one who protects and exposes evil and/or an Esther, called to be brave and take a risk in order to accomplish something great?

- Have there been times in your life when you have had to go "undercover?" Are you willing to step out if God gives you the opportunity?

DAY 17

ROE V. WADE: OVERTURNING THE ROOT OF ABORTION

**"Before I formed you in the womb I knew you,
before you were born I set you apart."**

— Jeremiah 1:5

One of the most amazing truths surrounding the birth of a child is the fact that each and every child has been issued a birthright at the point of conception. Our scripture in Jeremiah makes it very clear we are known by the Father before we are even formed. This is why the enemy fights so hard when it comes to the right to life. Remember in the book of Exodus when the Lord instructed Moses to apply the blood to the doorposts of every house where His covenant people resided? A death angel was going to pass through Egypt and strike down every firstborn child. Exodus 12:13 states, "The blood will be a sign for you on the houses where you are, and when I see the blood, I will pass over you." At midnight this word was fulfilled, and all firstborn children were killed, including Pharaoh's son. Every household in Egypt had someone dead within its four walls! But death passed over every house where the blood had been applied. Can you even imagine the horror of your household being cursed because of the king who ruled over your land! Pharaoh was so horrified that he summoned Moses in the middle of the night and ordered him to leave Egypt. He was to take all his flocks and herds and "get outta Dodge!" Next, I want to point out that Pharaoh said to Moses, "Also, bless me!" This is a very important statement, and we will come back to it.

Now I would like to turn our attention to another pivotal mass slaughter of life that took place. In Matthew 2 we read of wise men known as Magi. These men were looking for a boy whom they believed would become a ruler and shepherd for the people of Israel. Unfortunately they gave this information to the wrong person on their journey, a king named Herod (verses 1-2). Operating in a spirit of manipulation, Herod proceeded to ask the Magi to go and make a careful search for the child. As soon as they found Him, they were to report back so the king could worship Him as well (verses 7-8). After the Magi visited baby Jesus bearing gifts, an angel appeared to Joseph instructing him to take his family and leave because the Christ child had a contract put out on His life. Of all the places they could have been sent, it was back to Egypt—the very place of the original slaughter of the firstborn under Pharaoh's rule! An angel also instructed the Magi to take an alternate route home, and when Herod heard he had been outwitted, all hell broke loose. Unlike the first orders that came from God in the book of Exodus, this king had murder on his mind, and he gave the order that all firstborn males, age two and under, were to be slaughtered (verses 12-16). This time it wasn't by an angel of the Lord but by a man! Herod knew this baby, Jesus, would one day grow up and become king, so he had to be certain to kill him. He had no idea where this Savior was located, so every child had to go.

Currently our nation is in turmoil. Both the Democrats and Republicans are battling over key issues. Each party is casting dispersions upon the other, and an all-out war is ensuing. However, we must not lose sight of the real issue: a spirit of death from hell has been assigned to destroy life. I am about to explain why!

Donald Trump was inaugurated on *January* 20, 2017 as the forty-fifth president of the United States and stands firm as a pro-life president. On *January* 22, 1973, almost forty-five years prior to President Trump taking office, the U.S. Supreme Court ruled in Roe v. Wade that it is unconstitutional to violate a woman's right to choose to terminate her fetus.[1] Norma McCorvey, better known as "Jane Roe," remained anonymous for ten years; but after twenty-two years she gave her life to Jesus Christ and turned from being a pro-choice activist to being a pro-life activist! The miracle of this court case cannot be denied; the case took long enough to make its way through the courts that the decision did not come in time for Norma McCorvey to have an abortion. She gave birth to her child, whom she put up for adoption[2] in June of 1970. My God! The very fight was about her choice to take this child's life, but God protected the child. Her daughter's identity has never been revealed, and it is not clear if the now forty-seven-year-old woman knows she is McCorvey's daughter. That was the first time in history we saw a death warrant on a girl! There have been repeated challenges since 1973 to narrow the scope of this case, but the decision has never been overturned.

In *January* of 1993 former president Bill Clinton asked the FDA (Food and Drug Administration) to revisit the issue of an abortion pill that France had approved in 1988. On September 28, 2000 the FDA approved this pill "as a method of early medical abortion."[3] The prophetic time table cannot be overlooked. Ms. McCorvey didn't pass away during any other administration, but one month after President Trump took office, she died.

The Father began to speak to me regarding the prophetic placement of President Trump and godly Supreme Court Justices. Our president has been called by God, whether people want to believe it or not, as was Cyrus, king of Persia (Isaiah 45). The Bible tells us that Cyrus was anointed by God and was a deliverer of the Jews. It is important to also note it was President Donald Trump who historically moved the U.S. embassy in Israel to Jerusalem. In 2018 Israel celebrated seventy years of independence.[4] President Trump was seventy years old when he was inaugurated![5] One may question whether or not he was called, but the truth at hand is if he had not become president, you can be certain the person in office would see to it the execution orders of unborn babies remained in place! If you call yourself a believer in Jesus Christ, I would highly suggest you put your opinions of this man aside, stand with him in unity, and pray!

We are in a fight for life, my friends. We, as believers, know Jesus is coming back for His pure church. We cannot be blind to what must precede His coming. The intense political wars that are ensuing are a clear indication that deliverance is near.

The same spirit of manipulation King Herod used on the Magi can be seen in our day every time Democrats open their mouths. Just as King Herod cleverly asked the Magi to perform a careful search for the baby, so we witnessed the Senate demand a *careful and thorough search* of Judge Brett Kavanaugh's background. The plan was to manipulate and stall, because the Democratic Party knows that by placing this judge on the highest Supreme Court seat, abortion can, and will, be overturned eventually.

Remember when Pharaoh sent Moses away? He asked the very man he opposed through all kinds of sorcery to bless him (Exodus 12:32). The key point here is the harvest is ready! The very enemies we are fighting will eventually surrender when they witness the supernatural power of God. All your enemies will be amazed when they see God sweep through with His "executive orders," overturning unrighteous laws and restoring righteousness during President Trump's time in office. But as believers, no matter our political affiliations, it is vitally important that we all stand on the side of truth! While those who seem to be losing their minds need Jesus, will you be ready to apply the blood to the doorposts of their hearts so eternal death in hell passes them by?

The shaking of the White House, Courthouse, and now the church house is happening for one reason and one reason only: the saving of the lost! Who will the Democrats turn to, or who will your enemies turn to, when they are facing exposure of their sinful ways? Be available as a bridge, not a barricade. A barricade blocks a route. A bridge provides a link, connection, or means of coming together. We must be a bridge of hope to a dying world. Jesus is the answer this world needs!

No one knows the time of Jesus's return, but we must understand that the next generation of children to be born will be the ones who will lead a great end-time battle. Abortion has been the strategy of the devil since its inception because he knows *there will be a child born who will be raised up to command the army of God.* There may be many children, male and female, but Satan knows he must keep abortion in place because it is the "execution order" that gives him the best chance of killing the one or ones who will rise up as mighty warriors. Two evil leaders of the Bible, Pharaoh and King Herod, felt driven to execute the one in their times who could potentially steal their throne. When evil leaders rule the land, innocent people die because the leaders want to enforce their agendas above all else.

We are about to witness a great move of angelic hosts released upon the land to warn and instruct those who will listen. God is the same yesterday, today, and forever. He doesn't change; the mind-sets of people do. "Before I formed you in the womb I knew you, / before you were born I set you apart" (Jeremiah 1:5). No one can stop your destiny but you. Angels were on assignment even before you were born. Now you are set apart, as is the next generation, to bring in the harvest of souls and the coming of our Lord Jesus. We are so very close!

A CALL TO ACTION

- Make two columns below or in a separate journal. Title the first one "Father" and the second one "Mother." Fill in the columns by answering the questions on the next page.

A CALL TO ACTION CONTINUED

- Indicate deaths of family members on each side by abortion, murder, or sickness.
- Focus on the abortions, asking forgiveness on your behalf or theirs and canceling a spirit of death.
- List any "death patterns" you see passed down. Pray against those patterns or curses and speak life.

DAY 18

CONJUNCTIVITIS AND INFILTRATES: YOUR VISION IS ABOUT TO CLEAR UP

All of us, then, who are mature should take such a view of things. And if on some point you think differently, that too God will make clear to you.

— PHILIPPIANS 3:15

I have always had very good eyesight and have never had to wear glasses. It wasn't until I reached the age of fifty that I required reading glasses. Taking a shower is quite the fanfare because I now have to attempt to figure out, without my readers, which bottle is the shampoo and which is the conditioner. There are certainly times we can take our health for granted. Because my eyesight was always so clear, I never really put much thought into others' inability to see clearly.

An interesting situation arose during the writing of this book. I could not see for five days! At the onset I figured my eyes were very tired and strained from sitting at the computer for hours. Both eyes were watery, blurry, and eventually crusty in the morning. However, I noticed that my right eye seemed to be worse. When I really needed to focus, I counted on my left eye to see clearly. I would close the right eye and allow the left eye to do the work. Not only were my eyes hurting, but I began to suffer with headaches. Both my husband and I discounted all these symptoms and wrote it off to lack of good sleep. I continued to get up in the early hours to pray and seek the Lord; I just wouldn't read my Bible in the middle of the night because it hurt my eyes. My routine didn't change, even though it was obvious something was wrong.

One morning my eyes were so painfully red that I decided to run to the store to find an over-the-counter solution. When I found eye drops for pink eye, I assumed that was the problem. My daughters never had pink eye as children, so it never crossed my mind that could be the issue. With blurry vision and eyes half closed, I made it back home where I administered the drops to both eyes, but to no avail. My eyes showed no improvement. Intercessors were praying for me, as they knew this eye condition was holding me back from completing my book. My husband called to check on me, instructing me to get to the urgent care clinic as soon as possible. The doctor examined my eyes and informed me I was the second patient that day to come in with pink eye. Well there it was! I had pink eye. I made it to the pharmacy and purchased my two-hundred-dollar bottle of antibiotic drops, with an assurance by both the doctor and pharmacist I would feel relief within twenty-four hours.

The next day my eyes felt worse! I continued to pray for wisdom. All of a sudden, a brief thought came to mind. I had the sense to call the optometrist who had prescribed my reading glasses a few months earlier. With half-closed red, blurry, swollen, and crusted eyes, I made my way to the optometrist. I explained the story, and the first thing he asked was why I went to the urgent care clinic instead of calling him. Good question, isn't it? Hindsight is twenty-twenty vision! Pun intended! The optometrist proceeded to explain that the drops were making my condition worse because I had a viral infection, not a bacterial infection. He proceeded to explain the diagnosis was "infiltrates"! Immediately I had to curtail my enthusiasm because I knew the Holy Spirit was imparting supernatural revelation. I saw the doctor's mouth moving, yet I couldn't hear a word after he said "infiltrates." It was all I could do to get my new steroid eye-drop prescription filled and race straight home to my office. Even though I could hardly see, I could "see"!

The definition of *infiltrates* as a verb is "to secretly enter or join . . . in order to get information or do harm." *Infiltrates* can also be a noun that means "a substance that passes into the bodily tissues and forms an abnormal accumulation."[1] Infiltrates can be caused by either an infectious or noninfectious (sterile) condition; the latter being associated with contact lens wear, bacterial toxins, post-surgical trauma, autoimmune disease, and other toxic stimuli. The actual cause is relatively unknown.

I then researched pink eye, or conjunctivitis, which is an inflammation of the thin layer of clear tissue that lies over the white part of the eye and lines the inside of the eyelid. Children get this a lot, and it can be highly contagious because it spreads through day cares and playgrounds. Conjunctivitis is unlikely to damage vision if treated quickly.

The Holy Spirit made me totally aware of why this attack came upon me. He spoke to me clearly as I was looking into the mirror at my blood-filled eyes. At the exact time, he spoke the exact words to my husband. I am choosing to keep the details of this revelation private. It is wise to search out why attacks come our way. I think some people feel asking God why reflects a lack of respect or surrender to Him. I have always asked the Lord questions when something is happening because by the asking I've received incredible wisdom. I heard the Holy Spirit tell me that His body has been infiltrated. The members' ability to see clearly has been compromised, and they have crossed over into enemy territory. They run to certain people in ministry for answers and have received "one-size-fits-all" answers to their trials. In doing so, the wrong prescription has been administered, causing unnecessary prolonged pain that results in blurred spiritual vision.

We tend to ignore the warning signs our bodies are giving us, and we chalk them up to routine. When I began suffering with my eyes, I continued with my normal routine, discounting the warning signs that were so evident. I ran to the wrong person for advice and relief, when all along the eye specialist held the answers. I wasted time, money, and energy seeking out a prescription that in the long run was the incorrect solution to my existing problem. I assumed the first drops were the correct solution, when all along they were making my vision worse. Medical doctors and optometrists were both on my in-network provider list. Being accustomed to a familiar response prompted me to call on the medical doctor.

I have often heard preachers say that titles don't matter, and some pastors have gone to great lengths to become "hang-out" buddies with their church members. I have witnessed people calling their pastors by their first names as if they were best friends. Respect and honor quickly diminishes, resulting in church members becoming so familiar they are now unteachable due to the familiarity that has been woven into the relationship. Abuse of those in authority has resulted in this buddy system, but we must get back to God's order. Ephesians 4:11-13 says, "Christ himself gave the apostles, the prophets, some the evangelists, the pastors and teachers, to equip his people for works of service, so that the body of Christ may be built up until we all reach unity in the faith and in the knowledge of the Son of God and become mature, attaining to the whole measure of the fullness of Christ." I naturally assumed the urgent care doctor was fully qualified to diagnose my symptoms, when all along I had the optometrist at my disposal. Although the urgent care doctor certainly had my best interest at heart, the other doctor specialized in my particular condition.

The five positions in the Ephesians passage are set up to lead the body into orderly conduct until we reach maturity. Just as pink eye can be spread easily through playgrounds of children, so it is with the infiltration of the body of Christ. Churches have become playgrounds of disorder and disrespect, resulting in members of the body of Christ walking around with blurred vision. Many precious pastors are treated as if they are disposable: "I'll get rid of you and get another one just like you" mentality. We run from prophet to teacher to pastor for what pains us without being referred to the One who specializes in the answers. Imagine if my urgent care doctor had told me that my condition appeared to be pink eye, but she referred me to the specialist. I wouldn't have suffered for those weeks. I would have been out of pain a lot sooner, and I wouldn't have "sowed" the two hundred dollars in the wrong place! The apostle Paul told the Philippians that maturity should cause them to view things a certain way, but if they lacked that ability and thought differently, it would be made clear (3:15). If only I had slowed down and thought through what was happening to me. I would have avoided unnecessary pain. Because my eyesight was so affected, I paid more attention to the leading of God. Eventually my blurred vision cleared up, causing me to think differently!

We are about to witness the correction of the church's blurred vision. We will "see" it begin within those five positions of leadership. Jesus will remove those who are infiltrating the pulpits and spreading "religious conjunctivitis" throughout the body of Christ. When marriages need counseling, prophets will no longer prophesy to simply make the parties feel better but refer them to the pastor who will watch over and counsel them appropriately. Thus, instead of applying a prophecy bandage to the problem, the parties will be challenged to follow through with instructions their pastor shares with them.

Just as white blood cells mobilize to fight off infection within our bodies, we will also witness a great gathering of leaders who will chase out all terrorists, both foreign and domestic, from the body of Christ. The result will be a pure bride, just as prophesied throughout God's Word. The Great Optometrist is about to bring everything into focus! If your body has suffered attack, be encouraged! God will make the purpose of the attack clear to you! I understand there are times we may not understand, but I do believe we are entering into the times of a great unveiling of the enemies plots and purposes. No longer will the church suffer from blurred vision. We are all about to see in a way we have never seen before!

A CALL TO ACTION

- Are you dealing with sudden physical irritations or illnesses? If so, list them.
- Ask God if there is an emotional or physical correlation.
- Have you received advice from a leader or specialist that has caused trouble for you rather than helping?
- Ask God to lead you to the right doctor or Christian leader to get the problem solved.

DAY 19

BIPOLAR DISORDER AND MENTAL HEALTH

We will not hide them from their descendants, we will tell the next generation the praiseworthy deeds of the LORD.

— PSALM 78:4

I believe that somewhere along the way we have lost the tradition of sharing deep truths with our children. Life has shifted from the slow lane to the fast lane, allowing very little time, if any, for family devotions and teaching. Our scripture reading today declares that we will not "hide" these teachings from our children; and yet it's evident the mental state of this generation proves something is missing. I would like to encourage everyone to read this psalm in its entirety, because within the psalms are great truths concerning the outcome of our children should we fail to heed them. I would venture to say many of us have fallen short in this area. Many factors inhibit our inability to share focused family time, and yours may be different from what mine were I was when raising my daughters. One fact remains: children are headed for trouble if we don't take action now. It is too late to begin once all of your children are grown and gone. However, it's never too late to schedule regular family time if they are still living at home. Everyone has busy schedules, and they will always vary depending on activities, school, and work. Your family Bible time may change as needed, but it's important to schedule this time on a consistent basis. This shows your children that their mental, emotional, and spiritual health is a top priority!

According to the DBSA (Depression and Bipolar Support Alliance) more 5.7 million people suffer from bipolar disorder.[1] This disorder was formerly labeled "manic disorder," however the medical community has broken it down to four different levels. A manual called the DSM (Diagnostic Statistical Manual) was created in order to assess the severity of the symptoms. Bipolar disorder can be diagnosed at any age. The symptoms include radical mood changes, highs and lows that range from isolation to extreme high-risk behavior, feelings of awkwardness, being distracted easily, and slow to fast speech, to name a few. In order for a person to qualify for hospitalization, he or she must exhibit extreme or dangerous behavior that puts themselves or others at risk.

Bipolar disorder is a serious problem affecting celebrities like Charlie Sheen,[2] and Demi Lavato[3] to name a few, and possibly even your own family members. Recently, Kate Spade,[4] a well-known fashion designer, and Robin Williams,[5] a famous actor and comedian, both took their lives after suffering many years. The negative stigmatism attached to this disorder, as well as other mental health issues, keeps people from reaching out for help. Demi Lavato, who suffers from self-cutting, heroin abuse, and eating disorders states that medicating works for her. On June 21, 2018, she relapsed.[6] There has to be an answer to the epidemic that is assaulting our families, and as Christians it's our responsibility to seek out the answer! This devotional is for anyone who suffers with bipolar disorder but you believe that living the rest of your life with this disease isn't an option for you. You have had a sense all these years that there must be a way to be free and returned to your right mind. I believe that's exactly what you will experience! Freedom!

I had the privilege of being mentored by one of the greatest modern-day apostles of God to grace this earth, Harold R. Dewberry PhD. He was ahead of his time when it came to teaching about the inner transformations of the soul. In 2016 heaven gained another soldier who joined the "great cloud of witnesses" (Hebrews 12:1). Brian and I were heartbroken when for financial reasons we were unable to attend his funeral service. We had left Southern California and moved to Northern California six months prior. However, the Holy Spirit reminded me of his final words to me at his bedside. I had just listened to a teaching from a well-known megachurch pastor who refused in an interview to state emphatically that homosexuality is a sin. He danced around the subject, informing the interviewer that all were welcome in his church. Harold Dewberry was used to his firecracker spiritual daughter, so it didn't surprise him when I sat next to his bedside and furiously described the interview. His wife then cautioned me to not speak against God's anointed. I had no idea what Dr. Dewberry said next would be his final words imparted to my spirit: "Never compromise truth, Gina, but stand up for it." Looking back, Brian and I knew we had said our goodbyes that day in the hospital.

I was privileged to preach alongside Dr. Dewberry in a tiny church of about forty members. Many of them were plagued with mental illness; and yet Sunday after Sunday, with little financial compensation, he taught from his wealth of knowledge concerning the subject of mental health. I would go to his office where he would counsel those suffering with addictions or diagnosed with bipolar disorder, schizophrenia, and more. More than 80 percent of Dr. Dewberry's patients couldn't afford to pay, but that never stopped him. I was a witness to many who were set free and restored to their right minds!

I learned from Dr. Dewberry that while it is the soul of the person that has suffered the trauma, counseling requires careful discernment because we have to deal with the spirit of pharmakeia (from the Greek *pharmakeia*, word 5331 in Strong's,[7] from which we get our English word "pharmacy.") First and foremost we must realize that after ninety days of taking a medication, that chemical compound becomes part of one's personality! Medication affects the way you think, react, and receive truth. I have a mission to help as many who will break free from all medications. I will repeat what I've stated before. I believe medications are intended for a season not as a lifestyle. If you find yourself today living a lifestyle that is dependent upon pharmaceuticals, then join with me in pursuing truth that can and will set you free!

Every person who has come to me desiring help has been set free. I listen and pray for wisdom but never diagnose or tell anyone what he or she should do. However, I have witnessed a pattern of depression and anxiety that has resulted in bipolar behavior. In some cases I discerned sexual abuse at an early age that was never properly confronted by a trained counselor.

I counseled a twenty-year-old man who was diagnosed as having bipolar disorder and prescribed lithium. Ten years later he was sitting in my office. His mother didn't want him off this medication, and I understood her reasons. She feared her son would regress back to psychotic behavior. It only took one session for me to get to the root of his issue. He had been molested when he was six years of age, which led down a road of rebellious behaviors, including smoking crack. When he returned home from a drug-filled weekend, he started exhibiting psychosis. His parents were at their wits' end and took him to a psychiatrist where he was diagnosed with bipolar disorder. His true personality remained hidden for those ten years he was medicated, until I suggested he return to his doctor. He said he wanted to be weaned off of the medication, and within two weeks he was free! I suggested Zija Supermix® and premium detox tea during the weaning process in order to flush the toxins and feed his brain omegas and nutrients. Several years later, this man is happy, healthy, and serving the Lord!

Pastoral and professional counselors must counsel from God's perspective (Colossians 1:9-10). They must be able to identify and articulate clearly the reason behind the suffering! Every case I counseled where bipolar disorder was diagnosed, it involved alcohol, weed, opioids, or some form of *pharmakeia* that only exacerbated the symptoms. This is why you hear me repeat myself regarding Christians drinking or smoking. Personally, I don't want to put my hands or lips to anything in this world that is being used as a tool to enslave someone else!

Another common denominator of those suffering with bipolar behavior cannot be overlooked. It is common that these people were raised by a mother who was domineering and a father who was passive-aggressive. I had recalled Dr. Dewberry teaching me this many years ago, and in my own counseling experience I agree and have seen this to be 100 percent accurate. When we hear the term *domineering mother* we picture her immediately as controlling, boisterous, and loud. But that stereotype is not accurate. Some women have been forced to take control in the family because the father has remained passive when it comes to raising the children. The father will make excuses for not following through or the extreme passive-aggressive father will actually sabotage his wife or child's well-being and success. Most chronically passive-aggressive individuals have three common characteristics: (1) They're unreasonable to deal with; (2) They refuse to take responsibility for the problems they cause while blaming others; and (3) They rarely express their hostility directly and continue to repeat their subterfuge behavior over time.

In Psalm 78:4-8 we are told the children grew to not believe in God or trust in His deliverance. This is a heartbreaking scripture to read. How many adults today don't believe God can heal them from this disorder?

> A stubborn and rebellious generation,
> whose hearts were not loyal to God,
> whose spirits were not faithful to Him. (verse 8)

THE HEBREW WORD FOR "SPIRITS" is *ruah*, meaning the "heart or mind."[8] Today's generations have learned to put their faith in medical physicians instead of the Great Physician.

As parents we have all made mistakes. Maybe we weren't raised around the dinner table, sharing the wondrous works of God and His spiritual truths that would guide our lives. We violate God's spiritual laws and then wonder why the suffering persists. It can stop now, and I know this to be true. In Zechariah 3 God told Satan that He took away Joshua's sin. Everything was going up in flames, but God snatched Joshua from the burning rubble (verses 1-5).

I am a living and whole example of a "brand plucked from the fire" (verse 2 NKJV). Generations of my family have suffered, and the patterns continue to this day. But this child grew to become a young woman who asked why. God granted me wisdom and insight to break the devil's hold on my family. I knew it would require exposing roots that many in the family didn't want to face, but someone had to be brave. Even before publishing this book, I reached out to specific friends and family members, but as of yet I have received no responses.

I understand the sensitivity that surrounds this issue, and every situation is different, but mental health begins with our families. We must return to family time around God's Word where there can be open discussions about what our children are experiencing. A consistent, safe environment should be provided where events and pressures of life can be discussed. We also understand that suffering is an undeniable part of the human life that none of us can avoid. How we deal with suffering, though, is the key to our mental health and the mental health of those whom we love.

We are not meant to live out our lives in condemnation but rather conviction. Conviction is a sign we are close to the truth! Conviction is God's way of bringing us closer to healing. I encourage you, or anyone you know who is suffering from this mental torment, to draw close to the One who really knows you and reach out to one person you can trust. Professional counseling is necessary; however, the breakthrough will come when the root is exposed. Do not allow fear to keep you from the truth, because when we know, receive, and apply truth, we can be set free!

A CALL TO ACTION

- Have you or someone you know been diagnosed with mental illness?
- Do you believe this is a lifelong diagnosis you must learn to live with?
- In your case is it possible your current medications are masking a trauma?
- If you answered no, are you willing to seek professional help to explore possible trauma?

DAY 20

SCARS AND WRINKLES: BODY DYSMORPHIA DISORDER

Leah's eyes were weak and dull looking, but Rachel was beautiful and attractive.

— Genesis 29:17 AMPCE

My heart is burdened greatly for the generations of young people who are growing up in the age of social media, selfies, and reality television. Even we, as adults, are bombarded by it. I know we've heard over and over, "Hollywood doesn't define us," but what about daily reminders from social media of what you looked like on this day two years ago, or the home you lived in, friends who surrounded you, or relaxing vacations filled with happy memories? Subliminal thoughts, images, and messages bombard our spirits daily, and yet I know we haven't grasped the severity of the impact this steady stream of information is having on the lives of this media-saturated generation.

I am no exception to this onslaught of yesteryears' memories. Personally I was dealt a reality check when I had a memory pop up on a social media page that featured a photo of my husband and me on a bike ride in Southern California. This memory captured our tanned bodies on an adventurous bike ride, complete with rock-hard abs of steel and beautifully striated deltoids. Shapely legs told the story of the many all-terrain mountain bike trails we tackled together. We had even taken our selfie strategically under a "Bountiful Street" sign. Immediately upon seeing that photo I could feel my spirit sink to the lowest low as I recalled the events of that day. As I was viewing these memories, I was sitting in a bedroom with no windows or fresh air to take in. Two and a half years earlier, we had lost everything. Devoted friends left, taking what they could from my home, along with their friendships and trust, leaving behind their opinions of what God must be doing and why He was doing it. All those wonderful memories—but all we seem to be left with are scars and wrinkles. Thank you, Facebook, for my "On This Day" reminder. Here is where it all truly begins, my friends, with what I call the intersection of faith and reason. Dear Lord in heaven, many of us have the faith, but what could possibly be the reason for *this*?

Ever so gently through the years I would hear the Father speak to me that scars were beauty marks in heaven and that angels bow down when they see the effects of the battles we have fought. With my spiritual eyes I began to see the angels in heaven bowing down as saints were ushered in. These saints didn't look like what the world would define as "beautiful," with soft exfoliated skin, silky hair, and manicured nails, eyelashes attached one by one, and Botox™ strategically erasing any hint of possibility of declaring one's age. No, in fact, these battle-tested saints were entering heaven's gates torn and battered. I saw men who had lost limbs in war, as well as their children by divorce or premature death, and women who had spent time on their knees instead of in front of the camera. Also present were housekeepers who had labored faithfully year after year, arranging antiwrinkle creams and perfumes, organizing the messes left behind, and cleaning the bathrooms of those who could afford a home. All of these had openings and cuts in the flesh that were portals for God's glory to shine through.

The world sees beauty in a very different way from the way heaven sees it. Even Jacob declared that Rachel had such beauty in contrast to Leah. He was so overwhelmed by her outward appearance that he offered his life and labor to Laban in order to obtain Rachel as his wife. Misunderstandings, hurt, and children were all birthed from the veil of what was considered beautiful.

I absolutely believe we all should look our very best. First, and foremost, we must take care of ourselves. I've always believed that when we look good and feel confident with our own bodies, the feeling then translates into how we feel about our total selves. When we're feeling confident, it's only natural to then perform well at whatever we're putting our hands to. When people don't take care of their bodies, it's quite easy to recognize they like to stay in the background. Most of these people don't want to be caught in a picture, even a group photo. So, again, I encourage you to look the best that you can. This life is about your destiny! Those who are confident (but not prideful) and those who exude a healthy mind-set will excel in life.

Second, as a married couple, we definitely should want to be healthy, handsome, or beautiful for our spouses. Look what Jacob went through and sacrificed simply because of the beauty he recognized in Rachel. For the singles who do nothing to get fit, but constantly declare their "Boaz" is on the way, I encourage you to truly ask the Holy Spirit to motivate and empower you to desire a fit lifestyle. You will attract what you are and what you represent. A sharp, on-point entrepreneur who wants to change the world will not be attracted to someone who sits around all day eating and watching television. This is common sense!

Body dysmorphic disorder (BDD) is not as rare as one would think. BDD is characterized by the obsessive idea that some aspect of one's own body parts or appearance is severely flawed. When someone actually receives this diagnosis medically, it's said that *the patient takes exceptional measures to hide or fix this body part*. In reality, the flaw has been completely exaggerated by the person with this disorder.

A twofold situation is going on in the body of Christ. In the natural we have become very much inundated with Hollywood's version of beauty. I know that some of our most beloved ministers

Photoshop their pictures before posting them on Instagram because this feature is readily available. Cosmetic surgery is the norm, even among believers. I have no issue with utilizing some of these cosmetic procedures, but when people have to fill their lips with filler so they can make fish lips in their pictures, a body dysmorphic disorder is in play. Again, this disorder involves resorting to exceptional lengths to alter your appearance.

I began studying some of the top doctors who were on television back in the day. I ordered books and learned a great deal from their education. The main topics were natural pathways to healing and natural remedies. However, today, many of these doctors' faces are filled with so much plastic that they appear to be wearing masks. What are we really masking? Why would the world even want to listen to our natural health solutions when we ourselves look so far from natural? We somehow feel that if our lips aren't fluffy and pursed out like a fish, then we aren't beautiful.

I truly don't understand why no one is addressing this issue. The Leahs of social media walk away from their phones feeling as if they are totally inadequate. What is "beauty," and where is the balance? We either lean so far to one side to say our body is a temple (1 Corinthians 6:19) or go to the other extreme, taking the apostle Paul's words out of context in 1 Timothy 4:8 that physical fitness is only of *some* benefit, as if it's the least important on a believer's priority list. We major on the "some" and throw out the rest!

Next, body dysmorphic disorder is indicative of someone who goes so far even to hide his or her body parts. Bruce Jenner—I refuse to call him by a female name because God created a man—is a perfect example of this disorder.[1] Of course it goes much deeper. The body of Christ may judge him for the extreme measures he's taken to become a woman; yet, aren't we guilty of the same thing, resorting to extreme measures to hide body parts we don't like? People are not expendable or recyclable. Every life matters and everybody matters. We cannot just cut each other off and throw each other away because we can't get along. I am convinced this is an epidemic in the church today.

We must be ever so careful about judging the world. Are we, too, glorifying the Rachels at the expense of the Leahs? Are we going to extreme measures to hide our own body parts or those of others because we have decided these body parts are severely flawed? Speaking specifically to those of us who lead others and are highly visible in social media, we must be very careful if we are presenting ourselves photoshopped and perfect (as the world deems perfect), because all we are doing is raising up a generation of body dysmorphic candidates. Today's younger generation is looking for authenticity. How can the church present itself as authentic while doing these things? What if we began revealing living evidence of our battles and our victories? The fact remains, we must be balanced and prayerful in everything.

Is it possible that Leah's eyes were dull and weak because of what she had lived through and seen with her own eyes? To some the "roadmaps" written upon our bodies are unattractive, but to God, they are proof we have journeyed through some difficult seasons. Maybe we should reconsider how we present ourselves to this generation. I would venture to say these scars and wrinkles are proof of a life well lived! It's something to think about.

A CALL TO ACTION

- Did you grow up comparing yourself to other siblings?
- List areas where you felt you weren't good enough, pretty enough, or talented enough.
- Are you taking extreme measures to cover up any of these areas?
- Are you constantly viewing others' pictures, or their lives, on social media or reality TV shows? Pay attention to how you're reacting to what you view.

DAY 21

CAN WE LOSE OUR MIRACLE?

"Now see to it that you drink no wine or other fermented drink and that you do not eat anything unclean."

— JUDGES 13:4

Hold up! I can almost hear those religious spirits shooting their arrows at this subject! Please don't skip over this message nor put up roadblocks in your mind. God's about to do something amazing in your life, and many times His instruction precedes miracles. Anytime we are about to move forward in our faith walk, if we choose to listen closely, the Holy Spirit will lay out a course of action for us to implement. The problem is, more often than not, we *hear* those exciting words, "Move forward" or "Your miracle season has arrived," yet we fail to heed the instructions that will ensure both our safety and success within that movement. I've heard it tossed around often in Pentecostal circles that someone was healed but then they "lost their miracle." This statement never sat right with me. It makes people question God, when their faith is already wavering, wondering if He really cares about their pain. Maybe God was never involved in that miracle in the first place? Let's say, for instance, someone comes to the altar with herniated discs accompanied by excruciating pain. The preacher lays hands on him and prays a prayer of faith; then the person runs out of the meeting singing and praising God, only to experience the same pain days later. Did he really receive a miracle? What went wrong? Did God not know what He was doing, or did we miss something? Oh, I know, it was staged so the preacher could make money off the miracle. I'm about to teach you how you can miss your miracle even after hands have been laid!

We read in the book of Judges about someone who was about to receive a miracle. It's interesting to note that she's not even mentioned by name; she is only referenced by her physical condition and to whom she was married: "A certain man of Zorah, named Manoah, from the clan of the Danites, had a wife who was childless, unable to give birth" (13:2). Can you imagine being referred to in this manner? We can only imagine the heartache this woman lived with in respect to barren hopes and dreams. But that was all about to change. Her "now" moment was upon her. All of those emotional years filled with shame and embarrassment were now facing heaven. This woman, not her husband, was visited twice by an angel of the Lord. She must have approached the altar many times because this angel made two points very clear. First, she had been sterile and barren, unable to conceive children (verse 2). Second, her current state was about to change. Strict instructions were attached to this miracle at the angel's first appearance. The angel went on to explain that the woman was about to carry a son; however, she was to drink no wine nor partake of any unclean food. The angel even went further and made it crystal clear what *not* to do with her son's hair (verses 3-5). She was not even allowed to take him to Fantastic Sams for a trim!

This woman rushed straight to her husband to share what had just taken place (verses 6-7). One of two things will result when we share our personal miracles or visitations. People will believe and may even help us conceive this miracle, or they will doubt and contribute to aborting the miracle. I have made this mistake of sharing visions and words from God, but I especially identify with this specific story. Not every vision is to be shared because it wasn't given to anyone else but you. This is where confusion and misunderstandings take place. As a matter of fact, the ones with whom I shared thought I was a certifiable nut job and even labeled me a false prophet. Praise God this woman's husband, Manoah, believed her report and was on board and excited! So much so he prayed and asked for further instructions on *how* to handle the miracle (verse 8). It is imperative we understand *what* Manoah prayed. He desired another visitation. He asked the angel of the Lord to teach him and his wife how to raise the boy, and what the rule, work, and mission of this promise would be. This man of God wanted to be taught how to keep, guard, care for, and protect their miracle!

Understanding why God is birthing a promise in us is of utmost importance. When we know and understand, will we not be more apt to handle with care the miracles God gives us? We want to do this right! We must follow through with obedience if our desire is to honor and care for the promise He's revealed to us. Because this woman was directed as to what to do with the boy's hair, I believe it's safe to assume that even appearances do matter! We can choose to drink what we want, slam down a few beers, smoke a few cigarettes or cigars, and eat hot dogs all day. But our bodies, these physical temples, are carriers of the Holy Spirit and speak of future prophecies. Yes, we carry both the glory and the promises that are being transported from heaven to earth. It's a privilege and an honor to represent Jesus!

The point I am making is that it's vital we pay close attention when we are spoken to concerning heavenly matters. If this woman had decided after that visitation from the angel to head to happy hour with her girlfriends for half-price chicken wings and wine, she would have lost the baby or the miracle. The miracle was implanted within her womb. Please hear what I am about to say. She would have walked that promise straight into happy hour where the abortion process would have begun! The angel made it clear that the son she was carrying possessed great purpose. This miracle child was even pre-named Samson by God. The woman didn't have the option to go to the internet and search for the most popular boy names of the year! Strict instructions preceded this miracle.

I believe we do not handle heavenly mandates with fear and honor because we don't realize who we really are or the potential of what we can actually carry. This woman didn't cruise through the drive-through for burgers or stock up on wine, because she was told she would carry a son who would *initiate* the deliverance of Israel. Her miracle wasn't the complete answer for Israel's deliverance but the beginning!

Would we be willing to abstain from all unclean foods, people, or even medications if we knew the miracle God was about to hand us would be instrumental in changing the world? Even the children we have already birthed are world changers; therefore, it is imperative that we receive and implement guidance from heaven on their behalf.

God's love is so overwhelming. Just like children who respect and honor their parents we, too, should strive with all our hearts to be obedient. Our walk with God is never about what we can or can't do; rather, it is about what we are willing to sacrifice in order to be all He is calling us to. Not all mothers or "glory carriers" are called to the exact same purpose. Comparing ourselves to others regarding how we eat, act, or live our lives will only place burdens upon us we were never intended to carry. Just as Manoah went before God and prayed for specific direction concerning his family matters, shouldn't we do the same? Ask for guidance concerning the rules, work, and mission surrounding your promise. Then act on the guidance you've been given. God's plans for you will not only be for the deliverance of your own family but for many generations to come.

Don't lose your miracle, because a great price was paid that you might carry what heaven has assigned on your behalf. The beauty of our salvation is that we each are free to work it out daily (Philippians 2:12). Just keep in mind, it is work! Anything that comes from God is valuable and must be handled with care. You're about to birth something only you can carry. Is what you're about to eat, drink, or put into your body going to help birth the miracle, or abort it?

A CALL TO ACTION

- Have you felt that God healed you in a specific area only to lose that healing?

- Has God given you specific instructions concerning a promise in your life? Have you followed through in obedience?

- Are your current choices going to help birth your miracle or abort it?

- Are there areas of your life where you could better represent Jesus?

DAY 22

HEALED DURING ACTIVE DUTY

Naaman went away angry and said, "I thought that he [Elisha] would surely come out to me and stand and call on the name of the LORD his God, wave his hand over the spot, and cure me of my leprosy."

— 2 KINGS 5:11

I fully believe God can miraculously heal us at any time and any place! I am an eyewitness to His healing, delivering power. Here is my story.

I began sneaking cigarettes during my junior high years because my mother left them out daily as she smoked pack after pack. This gateway drug then led to smoking weed, using cocaine, then smoking crack. My first overdose resulted in two straight days of partying and club dancing with my Christian friend. Ironically, we were attending the Baptist church and Billy Graham crusades by day and smoking crack by night.

The second night, after hours of drinking and dancing at a club, my friend and I decided to invite a Cuban drug dealer we met back to our apartment. (Side note: I had accepted Jesus as my Savior in sixth grade, but due to extreme physical and sexual abuse, this behavior was my way of escape. I was being played by the devil. We all have demons assigned to us—as well as guardian angels—but I was an especially easy target for "the dark side" because I chose to open myself up to drugs.) Apparently, on this night in particular, the devil had plans to take me out. We were all smoking crack, when all of a sudden, my body was thrown into violent convulsions. My shocked friend was sure it was all over for me when she saw me swallowing my tongue and my eyes rolling back in my head. In desperation she began crying out to Jesus and asking Him for help. Miraculously, she said, she heard Jesus dictating step-by-step instructions to her: hold onto my tongue and begin filling up pots and pans with cold water to start dousing my face. To add to the mayhem the smoke detectors all went off! So I was convulsing on the floor, my friend was trying to hang onto my tongue while screaming for the Cuban dealer to hurry up with the water, and the smoke alarms were blaring. It must have been quite a scene.

As my friend doused my face with pan after pan of cold water, while frantically praying I didn't die right in front of her eyes, the dealer started smashing the smoke alarms because the last thing we wanted was for the police or fire department to show up. In the midst of this chaos, they had no idea I was experiencing a supernatural one-on-one encounter with Jesus, the Lamb of God Himself! We were walking hand-in-hand in heaven. I was feeling overwhelming love and mercy emanate from Him, and I saw people I recognized smiling and enjoying themselves; it was peaceful and beautiful. We could see straight past the body and into each other's spirit! But suddenly I bolted up from the floor in nothing short of a ferocious rage. I began cursing and swearing and ordering the dealer out of our apartment. He scrambled to gather up his belongings as fast as he could, flushed everything down the toilet, and dashed out the door.

As I came to my right mind and calmed down, I saw my friend standing in front of me. She looked as if she had just seen a ghost. She recounted everything that had just happened and said that after I had come to and was yelling and cursing, she saw what she described as a "demon" fly out of my mouth. The rage was not a result of my encounter with Jesus but rather the war between darkness and light being waged over my life! I was immediately in perfect peace and never touched crack again.

The second overdose occurred sometime later. I had heard that a teacher from my teen years was leaving town and would be renting his place out for three months. So my friend and I decided to grab it. One day while cleaning the house, we discovered a gram of cocaine stashed in a ceramic figurine. So, of course, we did what any saved/delivered/set-free believer would do—we snorted the cocaine! That little bit was all I needed, and the cycle began yet again. I knew just who to contact to get more.

One night I was alone in my bedroom and snorted a major amount within an hour. That amount should have kept me awake for days, but I fell asleep. Another visitation with Jesus took place. But this time He wasn't the Lamb of God, full of grace and mercy. He walked me around heaven, pointing out several groups of people from around the world. I knew some of them, and others I had never seen before. I was instructed to tell my story to them. Most of these people I knew had no idea I lived this kind of conflicted lifestyle, but Jesus still challenged me to come clean and tell everyone my story. What? What happened to the comforting Lamb of God? I was standing face-to-face with the Lion of Judah who was not pleased with me and was warning me that I had better shape up!

Let's fast-forward two years, when I was twenty-one years old. Working as an aerobics instructor and personal trainer, I had been clean for two years and had met a wonderful man at the gym where I was employed. I brought him to the Lord, and within a year we were engaged to be married. I decided to make a quick visit to my former cocaine dealer to tell him the good news of how Jesus had set me free from addiction, that I was engaged to be married, and everything was going great. After sharing my news with him, he offered me a tiny bit of cocaine. Overcome by the temptation, I scooped it up under my acrylic pinky nail and snorted! No big deal, right? Guess how that worked out for me?

(Refer back to Day 8, "Exercising and Exorcising Leaping Demons.")

I took off down the sunny California freeway in my white convertible that sported my license plate FIT4HIM, excited about my bright future, when out of nowhere, *BAM!* Excessive sweating and heart palpitations hit, followed by numbness that traveled down the left side of my body! I thought I was having a heart attack! I could see the Seal Beach exit just ahead. *Can I make it in time to find a hospital? No. I am going to pull over.*

There was no heavenly hand-in-hand this time; this one was all on me. I turned off the engine and bowed my head. The humility that came over me was like nothing I had ever experienced. Cars whizzed by, as I asked God to forgive me for blatantly disregarding my prior experiences with Him. I asked Him to bring a good woman to my fiancé. I was expecting to die right here on the 405 freeway at the exit I had taken so many times to hang out at the beach. But instead, to my surprise, my heart returned to its normal rhythm, the numbness left immediately, and the pain stopped. I had been healed instantly by the Great Physician! Just like Peter, I had denied Him three times. I never touched those drugs again!

Over the next fifteen years I began suffering more and more with migraine headaches, as well as lower back pain with a pinched sciatic nerve, caused by two herniated discs. I took various doctor-prescribed pain medications until I found myself addicted and unable to function without them. I had no idea that in reality I had become addicted to synthetic heroin. In desperation I reached out to pastors, friends, and prayer groups, hoping someone could give me advice as to how to wean off of medication or perhaps pray that God would heal me instantly. I detailed portions of this story in Day 10, "Finally Out! How to Beat Addiction," explaining the agonizing process of weaning off of these medications.

Fast-forward to 2015. One morning after Brian and I had left Southern California, I awoke to excruciating pain in my left shoulder and was unable to lift my arm. I had suffered a rotator cuff injury ten years prior, but for some reason on that particular morning the old injury decided to rear its ugly head. I kept expecting the pain to subside, so I fought through it for a few weeks until I finally decided to call a doctor and schedule an MRI. Would you like to guess what he prescribed for me during this process? You guessed it—the same pain pills I had been delivered from five years earlier. Surely God understood that I needed relief until surgery could be scheduled. But, to my surprise, the very medications that were supposed to help me feel better actually worked against me, causing panic attacks and symptoms of withdrawal. I recalled that Dr. Harold Dewberry explained how this was possible, how the medications eventually work against you, magnifying the very reason you took them in the first place! Proverbs 26:11 flashed through my mind many times that week: "As a dog returns to its vomit, / so fools repeat their folly."

After much prayer Brian and I decided to go ahead and schedule the surgery. The day of the surgery finally came. With Brian at my side, I was lying on the gurney in my hospital gown, ready to be wheeled into the operating room, with an IV in place. The nurse was telling me what I to expect; following the operation the pain would be intense, so I would need to fill my prescription for pain pills immediately. She recommended taking them consistently for at least a month. All of a sudden, what I can only describe as a righteous fear rose up inside of me. I sat up and started ripping off the tape holding the IV in place and pulled the IV out of my arm! The astonished nurse wasn't sure what to do. The doctor walked in, and they both attempted to reassure me this surgery was necessary. I would continue to suffer pain if I didn't have the surgery. Meanwhile, my concerned husband, thinking I was experiencing a "fight or flight" moment similar to what fighters experience just before a fight, was trying to encourage me to go ahead with the surgery. He didn't want me to leave the hospital with a torn rotator cuff. But I told him God was definitely speaking to me, "Get out now!" So he trusted me, helped me put my street clothes back on (which I was picturing as armor!), and we walked out of the hospital door.

I share my story vulnerably because, just like Naaman, God had to deal with my flesh. In 2 Kings 5 we read that Naaman was a commander of high esteem in the Syrian army; but there was one problem—he had leprosy (verse 1). Everyone knew the long-term effects of leprosy were devastating to the point that a person must eventually live isolated from his or her work, family, and friends. One day the Israeli servant who worked for Naaman's wife told her that there was a prophet of God living in Samaria who could heal her husband of this dreadful disease (verses 2-3). So this proud man had it all figured out! Naaman with all his horses and chariots rode over to Elisha's house (verse 9). Elisha sent out a messenger who told the commander, "Go and wash in the Jordan seven times, and your flesh shall be restored and you shall be clean" (verse 10 AMPCE).

Naaman was highly insulted that he came all this way only to be met by a lowly messenger and not the prophet! What kind of crazy instruction is this? "I thought [Elisha] would surely come out to me and stand and call on the name of the LORD his God, wave his hand over the spot and cure me of my leprosy. Are not . . . the rivers of Damascus, better than all the waters of Israel? Couldn't I wash in them and be cleansed?" (verses 10-12). Naaman was ready to take off, but thankfully his servants talked him into giving it try, and Naaman was indeed healed (verses 13-14).

As I said at the beginning of this devotional, God can and does heal people miraculously! However, getting to the root of what is causing our illnesses and diseases is most important. In my case I had injured my shoulder at an earlier time and had experienced pain on and off for the ten years until the episode in 2015 that drove me to a doctor. This experience succeeded in showing me that I absolutely could not go back to the addictive drugs and there had to be another way. God allowed me to experience the danger and side effects of medications. He wanted me to die completely to my flesh in the area of addiction and walk out the long process.

Naaman thought that because of his position with the king, he would be entitled to a personal audience with the well-known prophet. He thought he could whip out his checkbook, have the prophet wave his white coat over him, and be healed instantly. After this meeting, they could go kick back at the Samaritan Suites for a celebratory drink. Fortunately for us, most of the time God has something more creative and far-reaching in mind, and we must die to our pride and preconceptions. Because this Syrian commander humbled himself and was obedient to the word of Elisha, he was healed. And when he walked from the Jordan River back to Elisha's house Elisha was waiting for him. "Now I know that there is no God in all the world except in Israel . . . your servant will never again make burnt offerings and sacrifices to any other god but the LORD" (verses 15-17).

The day I pulled the IV out of my arm, got dressed, and walked out of that hospital with my husband, God healed me instantly! I have an MRI scan to prove it! This warrior in God's army can testify to saying *no* to my flesh and to what made perfect sense in the natural and saying *yes* to the God who can heal the inside and all the way out.

Now it's your turn to be healed during active duty.

A CALL TO ACTION

- As a parent or grandparent, do you have anything in your home that could be a stumbling block to children? Can Jesus walk through every room in your home, open every drawer and approve?
- Schedule a "clean house" day, asking for wisdom in each room, including your children's.
- Has God delivered you from something, but you are attempting to justify why you've returned to it?
- Pay attention to sickness in the home or bad attitudes, and note changes since you "cleaned house."

DAY 23

WORDS ARE WEAPONS: ADULT CHILDREN OF ALCOHOLICS

The tongue also is a fire, a world of evil among the parts of the body. It corrupts the whole body, sets the whole course of one's life on fire, and is itself set on fire by hell.

— James 3:6

Have you ever heard the sayings, "Don't speak until you are spoken to," or "Children should be seen and not heard"? We know that words have the ability to create and deliver, but they can also usher in death. In Genesis 1 we read that by the very words of God everything was spoken into existence. Proverbs 18:21 tells us that our tongues hold the power of life or death. You have probably heard this said many times, but I want to bring to your attention *how* a word actually travels and can become a word curse!

I've always been a *why* person. Many times we are advised not to ask why but to accept what's been handed to us and walk through it prayerfully. Through the years I have gathered quite a bit of wisdom by trying to figure out why a particular situation is happening, which has helped me understand its effect. According to Newton's Third Law, which says that for every action, there is an equal and opposite reaction, and with every cause (a person or thing that makes something happen [or exist] or is responsible for something that happens) there is an *effect* that *affects* (moves someone emotionally)! The root of much of what we suffer today can be traced back to *words*! As I approach life with this perspective, I've had to be careful not to judge, but rather objectively assess one's state in order to bring truth and healing into his or her life. My experience has been that when dealing with healing and deliverance ministry, the root cause of someone's physical symptoms could be traced back to something someone said or the actions someone took. Matthew 18:34 declares that harboring unforgiveness invites tormenting spirits. Many believers have left themselves wide open to the devil's schemes by failing to "release" the words or criminal act perpetrated against them. Every action, or lack of action, we take will result in some type of physical manifestation.

Back when I was in grade school, a portion of the school's property was set aside for the special needs children. I can recall swinging on the monkey bars, showing off my ability to cleanly execute the "death drop," which was a popular gymnastics move on the high bar. Everyone would be fascinated as they watched the bravest child jump to the highest bar and perch on top. Leaning back I would perform a half-circle swing without hands and, hopefully, land on my feet. I suppose I was a leader at a young age when it came to athletic ability. Coming from a home of word curses that were served daily, I enjoyed the attention I received for my death-defying stunts. Then, before the bell would ring, I would make my way over to say hello to the other children who were kept isolated from the rest of us. I could hear my friends yelling out demeaning words to these kids. So I would then run back over and sock them in the face. Looking back, I understand my passion was created as a result of the hurtful words I endured before school within my own house. This non-focused anger, which was really unresolved hurt, became fuel to save those who could not save themselves. I never wanted anyone to have to experience the pain I was feeling from reckless words.

Let's turn our focus to the portion of today's scripture that says that words "corrupt the whole body, sets the whole course of one's life on fire."

Shortly after Brian and I were married, he was sitting on the edge of the bed. As I frequently do, I took his head in my hands to pray for him. This day something very different happened. As I opened my eyes I witnessed his jaw begin to lock up. I didn't know if Brian was in the Spirit or suffering some odd sort of pain. I asked a few times if he was OK, but there was no response. I continued to pray over him in the Spirit, and I began to notice tears streaming down his rugged face. I would estimate this went on for about thirty minutes. Finally, Brian was able to recount what happened, and I realized that heaven graciously touched us with wisdom that would change everyone who heard this story. Brian explained that when I began praying, he felt extreme pain in his heart, and then it traveled up the right side to his jaw. His jaw began to lock up as the pain made its way to the right side of his brain. This is why he could not answer me!

Revelation began to pour forth as Brian recalled a childhood memory that had been *locked* away. He told me when he was a young boy he always asked his stepfather a lot of questions, as any inquisitive child does with his father. But one day, Brian's stepfather's tongue turned into a weapon. Irritated with his son's constant inquisitiveness, he looked over at Brian and said, "Why do you always ask so many stupid questions?" That was the day Brian stopped asking for help and the questions ceased. As you can imagine, school became a huge challenge for Brian because he refused to ask the teachers any questions for fear of sounding stupid. Everything Brian attempted became extra difficult because he chose not to ask for help. But he always found a way to navigate through every challenge that was thrown his way. In that instant, I understood Brian, and everything began to make sense. We are more accepting of one another when God unfolds events that have shaped our character.

Brian never knew his biological father; in fact, one day he overheard a conversation between his mother and stepfather. He overheard his mother say, "You treat him like this because he's not your own." There is a common denominator among warrior men; they were not raised by their fathers. His stepfather was a kindhearted man but became overcome with anger when he drank. Unfortunately, he passed away at the young age of forty-five due to his alcoholism. It's important to understand that children of alcoholics learn to maintain control over their feelings and behavior so as not to "push the wrong buttons" of the alcoholic. It is not uncommon for them to bury their feelings (particularly anger and sadness) and have a difficult time feeling or expressing emotions. Ultimately, they fear all powerful emotions, even positive emotions such as fun or joy. Quite often they misinterpret assertiveness for anger, therefore causing them to seek the approval of others while losing their identities in the process. Frequently they isolate themselves.

If you grew up in an alcohol-driven environment, you may have "triggers" (a stimulated memory) surfacing in your mind now. Freedom comes when we begin to understand why we are wired a certain way. We do not have to live as products of our dysfunctional environment! God allowed you to walk through all you have experienced in order for Him to receive the glory as your soul is set free. You are then free to go and help others with the same comfort and wisdom you received from the Father (2 Corinthians 1:3).

The brain is divided into two equal hemispheres: the right and the left. The right side is responsible for creativity, awareness, imagination, *intuition*, insight, holistic thought, music awareness, *3-D forms*, and *left-handed* control. The left side responds to analytic thought, logic, language, reasoning, science and math, number skills, and right-handed control. Although equal in size, these two sides are not the same, and most certainly do not carry out the same functions. Brian is left-handed, and he was shut down in the areas of intuition and imagination! The words spoken to him when he was a child formed a weapon that pierced his heart. While I was praying, the memory created pain, locking his jaw and resulting in pain on the right side of his brain! An interesting fact about Brian is that his secret weapons in the octagon ring are his jab and left hook. The very weapons fashioned against him are now his deadly weapons against the enemy himself! God is to be praised because Brian is one of the best communicators I know. He is stable and even-keeled. He was destined to relive the same destructive patterns he learned. But Brian chooses not to drink and has learned to confront issues by communicating, even if others don't reciprocate.

I am on a mission to encourage people to seek spiritual help and counseling first, rather than a doctor, for pain. What if we are missing deep healing truths that God is attempting to reveal to us? Are we correctly *applying* the revelation hidden within the scriptures? "It is the glory of God to conceal a matter, / to search out a matter is the glory of kings" (Proverbs 25:2).

Words have the ability to corrupt the whole person. "Word weapons" may have already set a negative course for you, but you possess the power and ability to course correct and turn your life around!

A CALL TO ACTION

- Has someone spoke a word to you that's been crippling? Identify the word(s) and how you reacted.

- List actions you can take to deal with the negative words.

- Did one or both of your parents drink alcohol? If the answer is yes, has it affected you? How?

DAY 24

EYES WIDE OPEN: WHO WILL SPEAK ABOUT WHAT THEY SEE?

My mouth will speak words of wisdom;
the meditation of my heart will give you understanding.

— Psalm 49:3

Brian and I were in the midst of an extremely stressful season. Sometimes we would treat ourselves to a cold, creamy ice cream cone and a relaxing walk at a nearby park. The sounds of children laughing, the merry-go-rounds spinning, and families spending time together filled the atmosphere. I carry such a great love for people that most of the time I can't turn off the prophetic insight. All five of my senses are so keenly aware of everything going on around me that in order to turn off the insight, I need to be alone; but we were living with others at that time, so we made our way outside for some fresh air.

My husband and I are good at withdrawing in order to be alone with each other and refresh ourselves in the Holy Spirit. However, during this season in our lives we found it almost impossible. This particular day was one of those spiritually heightened days when I just couldn't turn anything off. I began to observe everything going on around me. Without exaggeration, I noticed that 90 percent of the parents in the park were grossly overweight! In addition to this observation, I noticed they were on their phones and eating or drinking while their children played. I'm in no way being judgmental, just simply assessing the future of this next generation. I also couldn't help but wonder how much time these parents would have to raise their children, let alone grandchildren. Those young parents were only in their late twenties to mid-thirties, and I wondered what their families would look like when the children became preteens. The parents appeared exhausted and obviously possessed no energy to play with their children. Even more troubling were the children themselves. They, too, were very overweight. Some were eating hot dogs or candy and drinking soft drinks. If we saw a child drinking a beer in that park or doing drugs, we would certainly speak up and take action. Well, *some* of us would take action. My question is this: Where is the concern for the child who will most likely end up being diabetic from all the sugary drinks and having ADHD (Attention Deficit Hyperactivity Disorder) from all the dyes they contain?

ADHD is a mental health disorder of the neurodevelopmental type. The child or adult has difficulty paying attention, and his or her behavior can exhibit little or no regard for consequences as well as having trouble regulating their emotions. When someone's nerves are affected, it can most often be traced back to a trigger, such as a traumatic event and yes, even food![1] Many people are told they suffer from PTSD, ADHD, and a variety of other labels; and medication is generally the first go-to for help. We must begin to examine our own situations before running toward medications. In regard to diet being the main culprit, hot dogs contain carcinogens that are proven to cause cancer![2] I wanted to yell at the top of my lungs to anyone who would listen to me, "Why is your overweight five-year-old eating cancer-causing food? Can you tell me why there's blue dye all around your child's lips? You do understand the doctor diagnosed him with ADHD, right? The dye is the terrorist!" Can someone speak up with me? Am I the only one who sees this as child abuse? When a stranger abducts a child from a swing, everyone yells for help. However, the very food you place in your child's hands can also harm him or her. We are slowly allowing food to abduct our children. Yes, I was enjoying a delicious ice cream cone. Most likely the only one I had all summer. Everything must be done with moderation and balance, but where is the line between balance and being diagnosed with a disorder? We take our children to the doctors who prescribe medications because their brains are overactive. They can't sit still nor can they pay attention; they become inattentive, hyperactive, or impulsive. But instead of eliminating unhealthy foods one by one from their diets, we medicate them!

I used to have a friend whom I spent time with on a daily basis because we both had young children. At the beginning of our friendship she was grossly overweight. I saw great potential in this woman as well as her son who was gifted prophetically (God will show me those I am to take the time to speak to and instruct). One day I decided to pay special attention to exactly what this child was eating and drinking as well as his activity level since we were together most of the time. You can spend so much time with certain people that you become desensitized to the very truth that is staring you in the face. Routines have a way of causing us to miss something because we settle into daily habits. The boy had not entered public school yet, so he was with his mother all the time. I noticed whenever my friend and I would get a coffee he would ask for a smoothie. Her answer was always yes, and he would be handed a frothy drink as tall as his little body. Almost every morning he would suck down a smoothie that was filled with whipped cream, sugars, and dyes. Then, at lunchtime, he had fast food "chicken" nuggets, fries accompanied by plenty of sugar-filled ketchup, and a soft drink. Between-meal snacks during the car drive could consist of any type of chips or crackers. I began to realize this sweet boy was receiving zero nutrition throughout the day. This mother loved her son so very much, and her way of showing it was to give him whatever his little heart and tummy desired. I shared with her what I was seeing, which opened her eyes to the dangers of this way of showing love.

The previous year I had counseled another family member,

which resulted in getting her off Ritalin. Afterwards some serious issues arose that never would have presented themselves had she stayed on this medication. Also, this mother's weight gain finally stopped when we got to the root of why she stuffed herself at 3:00 every afternoon. She had been a "latch key" child, and every day after school at 3:00 she ate because she was left alone. I have discovered once we begin peeling away the layers of the onion, people will either stay with me or go, depending on how badly they want to dig for the root issues. This peeling away didn't stop with her because I asked about her husband's compliments regarding all the weight loss. She told me he had not said a thing to her! How can a woman lose more than fifty pounds, begin working out at the gym for the first time, and yet receive not one compliment from her husband? I saw the detachment coming, and I knew I was going to have to go because too much change was hitting this family. I often wondered why so many people I have helped stopped contacting me, or to the other extreme, raged against me with hate and betrayal. It wasn't until I married my husband that I really understood. He explained that I see truth, and I want to help, but people only handle so much of it before they have to run the other direction.

My prayer is that revelations in this book will help you run as close to the flame as possible so purity can have its perfect work. Just like the day in the park, I see details that lead to truth. We become addicted to certain things for a reason, and it's vital that we figure out those reasons. When a person has an adopted child, drinks excessively even while on the job, views pornography, and has a slew of other issues, my first inclination is to shift the focus to the root of these behaviors rather than the "diagnosed disorders" that have led an entire family on a downward spiral.

One day, as I lay on my bed, I had a vision that I was standing in front of a person and sharing excitedly something the Lord had told me. My arms were moving as they always do when I am talking, and everything within me was so excited. However, I noticed the person was overwhelmed. I then felt the hand of Jesus gently take my chin and turn my focus to a huge arena. I saw a platform that was so large it couldn't be measured. Then He said, "The fire and power are now too overwhelming for one-on-one ministry." I understood what He was saying, and it was exciting but sad at the same time. I have only preached a few times in churches since then, but it has been made more and more clear to me that I am going to be preaching from a different sort of platform—this book!

I understand that some people will not agree with everything I am writing, but others will receive the revelation and understanding for which they've waited. We must ask ourselves why we do what we do and eat what we eat, and I believe every detail is wrapped up in God's Word. He will allow us to discover whatever it is we need to deal with. Then it's up to us what we are willing to do about it. But just like tears come as we peel away the layers of an onion, the closer we get to the center of the onion, or the root cause of our issue, tears will undoubtedly begin to flow. I believe the time has now come for believers to be willing to seek out counsel instead of masking symptoms with medication and food. When we attempt to cover up our own pain, and the pain in our families, we will affect others with whom we associate. I am witnessing this spread throughout the church with every family I have personally been involved with who rejects help.

Our scripture reading for today tells us the meditation of our hearts will grant us understanding. Then our mouths will speak forth wisdom. We must begin to understand our actions first before we can speak the answers to others. My friends, truth is right in front of our faces. The answers we need can be found by examining our own behaviors and the reasons behind them. Truth doesn't exist to bring condemnation; it brings freedom and liberty. Precious Christian families are suffering in silence. The suffering can end if we take each situation to the Lord and examine it before Him. If one is unable to break through, that person must be willing to seek out godly counsel.

The church is asleep, and God's about to wake her up! We've complicated so much of the deliverance process! We accuse others for our situation, or even God, because we have not experienced the deliverance we were promised. I heard the Spirit of the Lord say,

"They seek deliverance, but I am asking for discipline." James 4:1 says, "What causes fights and quarrels among you? Don't they come from your desires that battle within you?" We all want to be warriors in God's kingdom; however we must learn first to conquer our own battles. We eventually take these quarrels outside our own "ring" and enter into fights we have no business fighting! The body of Christ will no longer suffer from ADHD, because God's about to open the eyes of His bride.

A CALL TO ACTION

- Do you engage in activities with your children or grandchildren, or do you tend to sit and watch them play? Plan to join in on the fun!

- Have you or the children in your family been diagnosed with ADHD? If so, what are the signs surrounding this "diagnosis"?

- Are you willing to cut out all dyes and sugars and keep a journal of changes in behavior? If you are taking Ritalin, research the side effects.

- Ask for wisdom concerning any events that possibly surrounded this "diagnosis."

DAY 25

THE MIND-SET OF A FIGHTER

Caleb quieted the people before Moses, and said, "Let us go up at once and possess it; we are well able to conquer it." (Numbers 13:30 AMPCE)

— Numbers 13:30 AMPCE

I sincerely love surrounding myself with men and women who are fighters and warriors. They exhibit a keen, sharp attitude and carry a confidence that is undeniable in contrast with a person who is merely puffed up with his own ego. Anything is possible in a warrior's thought process, and resistance only confirms that what he or she is about to obtain will be worth the fear and danger along the way. Somehow, these fighters are fueled by the challenge. With their faith exercised, success as well as failure only builds, stretches, strengthens, and ultimately tests beyond what they could ever imagine on their own. The mind-set of a fighter is to learn to glean from losses, not wins, in order to never repeat the same mistake twice. God designed fighters with the capability of handling every single blow. The greater the output of faith against all odds, the more they will learn about the Father's character as well as their own, tapping into the revelation needed for the next part of the journey.

Do you suppose many people forfeit the prize because they stop short, or may I use the MMA term *tap out*, before the next level awaiting them? Such a radical faith is so evident in the face of clear and present danger that you can't help but know you're in the company of the elite.

This elite force of warriors is an uncommon breed that won't take no for an answer nor will they shrink back by what they see or hear from civilians who have never stepped out into this type of territory. They understand the common man fears the giants more than he can taste the fruit of the land flowing with milk and honey (Numbers 14:9). The warriors carry an innate ability to see what the common man is incapable of seeing. Let me interject here that it is important to be very careful not to judge or form offenses towards those who cannot go with you or comprehend what you're about to attempt. Their own personal warrior instinct, or lack thereof, will take them as far as they are willing and able to sacrifice. We all know we produce fruit from our hearts, whether broken or healed, and the final outcome will undoubtedly be a direct result of how we handle the offenses that attack our hearts.

I can recall the first year I moved out on my own with my daughters, while going through my divorce. I was used to being told by my ex-husband that I always had to have the best and that mediocre wasn't good enough for me. After years of hearing this, the concept began to trouble me deeply, and I started to question myself. Was I being prideful in my choices and mind-set? Why am I so motivated to strive for the very best in whatever I set out to do or purchase for myself or others? I have a dear kindred sister to my heart, and her name is Tami Barthel. This woman deserves to have a book written on her life story. She has been a loyal sister to me for more than twenty-five years. One day I told Tami what had been ingrained in me, and she began to share a story regarding her own children. Every time she put a catalog in front of her four children and told them to choose whatever they wanted, one child always, without fail, ordered the most expensive item. She explained to me that this was how God created her youngest son to always want the best, and that was OK. You see, those simple words set me free to understand that God made me the way I am, and it explained why everything I "chose" seemed to be of the highest quality and top-of-the-line best. I've always said I am anointed to make money and spend it! Meaning, give me a dollar and watch how far it can go!

Isn't that how King Solomon built his temple? First Kings 10 speaks of the queen of Sheba visiting the temple in awe of what Solomon had built as well as his skill and wisdom, but verse 5 indicates she lost her breath just noticing the clothing of servants, even the entry of the temple. I truly believe if Solomon was shown an Amazon website, he would've ordered only the best. God used all these things for His glory because, I believe, it was the mind-set He imparted within the very fiber of Solomon's character for multiple reasons. Therefore I, too, am at peace with this for myself. I pray more Solomons and queens are raised up in this coming wealth transfer so we, too, can cause the leaders of other countries to lose their breath and wonder about this mighty God we serve.

Every choice I make is honestly driven by how my choice could affect someone else positively or negatively. For example, each room of my home at the time reflected what I felt would minister to me as well as everyone who enters it. I removed the cheap plastic switch plates from every light switch and replaced them with some sort of artwork that had a scripture verse on it. Near the doors I displayed oil paintings or words that breathe life upon all who pass through. In the backyard I even purchased pieces of stone and laid them in a strategic order so everywhere my guests place their feet will lead them to the pool. The very first stone on the path is shaped like a heart!

Warriors, you are so unique in every way! We believe we can take the land and take others in with us. When I eventually purchased the home where my daughters lived before they took off for college, God challenged me in a way that most certainly required a warrior mind-set. You see, I wouldn't settle for a condominium, apartment, or pre-owned home. I refused to get a nine-to-five job and leave my daughters, for my mind-set was to continue providing the atmosphere my daughters were accustomed to. In the midst of the divorce I even strived to preserve what I had stood for spiritually. I wanted to be the one making the major decisions for my children's lives, and this is how warriors think. They do not settle. They use every rock and stumbling block hurdled onto their path, not to trip them up, but to take them higher. I wanted to make sure my girls felt comfortable inviting friends to our home. Now, I am not being a "name it and claim it" preacher here, but my purpose for this devotion is to impart to you a mind-set of courage. (Remember, your "land" may not be actual property, but it can represent many other victories God has already shown you.)

I happened upon a million-dollar property, and with the faith of my warrior friend, real estate agent, and a couple of other prayer partners, we began marching around the land and declaring this home for myself. Ridiculous offers were made numerous times, but the owner wouldn't relent. Remember, I didn't want a pre-owned home where another family had tread upon the carpet, and one day I saw the home! Brand new, custom homes were going up on the same block as the girls' private Christian high school. This story is amazing, and to God be all the glory for the great things He did for me! Every detail was overseen by Him, for answered prayer beyond belief took place in many arenas. But as I sat down to sign the contract to purchase this home, I looked down at the property description on the contract that said "Lot 38222" and curiously I asked my friend, "What does this mean?" She told me it was the lot number where my home was built. She knew where I was going with that question, because at 2:22 a.m. that very day I received a prophetic dream. I was taken on a death-walk straight to the gas chamber as thousands behind bars watched with great sadness and compassion. This prophetic dream was filled with details that would be a road map for my life, even to this day!

Listen, my friends, I had no job! I had been a stay-at-home mom, wife, and a homeschooling, Africa-preaching, crusade-launching mama, and I was ready to take my land! In today's scripture reading, Caleb had to quiet the people because they didn't believe. Thankfully, everyone I kept around me at the time believed with me, but can you imagine the doubters and haters all watching this transpire? I could hear them: "Just look at how she's spending her ex-husband's alimony and child support! It must all be going to the mortgage and not to the girls!" None of that is true.

Silence those around you, warriors! Take your land! We moved into this home in August 2008, and within the month a friend gave me a thousand dollars to buy some start up gym equipment. Oh, did I forget to mention this home had a four-car garage? What in the world did I need with such a huge four-thousand-square-foot property with a game room, custom pool that I added, cash, and all the other amenities? I'm glad you asked! The garage became the gym for The Word and the Workout, where I trained many from Homeland Security. In 2009 God spoke to me, "Truth-N-Love Ministry International," and this home also became the international ministry headquarters. Oh, go take that land warrior! We don't make sense to so many watching us, even to our own family members, and embracing challenges and danger only makes us appear even more ludicrous. Can I tell you the hundreds that were saved, baptized, housed and cared for, went through detox, were freed from prostitution, fed, loved on, and sent away full of hope, just by being in this home!

What are we fighting for? Why are we in the fight? Does something inside of you make you angry? Fighters see the atmosphere as a controlled atmosphere, where outside forces can't come in. It's you and your opponent. Life is full of distractions, and they come from many directions. A fighter has to have laser-beam focus; and, sometimes, even making it to the actual fight or event is a fight within itself.

A fighter in the physical realm has to map out his or her daily training. This is accomplished through grappling, boxing, kickboxing, counters, drilling, takedowns and submissions, and his shadowboxing. Alongside this training is the ongoing conditioning: running, cross-training, mountains, and hills. Changing up the terrain presents a mental fight in and of itself, knowing the challenge is always changing. The more a fighter is prepared for the day of battle, the less worried he will be because he took the time to prepare.

Every fighter must have an experienced coach who oversees all of the avenues, such as making sure the fighter does not under train or over train and understands that fighters will keep pushing past all limitations at any cost. More often than not, fighters don't always know when to stop. Unless a fighter is a seasoned veteran who learns to know his or her own body's limitations and weaknesses, injuries will be inevitable. Open communication with coaches and mentors is imperative, and a fighter must be able to trust and be vulnerable, open, and honest regarding both physical and mental struggles. True fighters will still continue to train and fight and learn to work around their injuries. "Excuses don't stop me from a fight or danger," says veteran in the MMA industry, Brian Warren. "Unless something is broken or torn, I am going in!"

Mature spiritual coaches and spiritual mentors will always encourage us to rest at the proper times and battle when necessary. Surrounding ourselves with quality leaders is vital in these end-time battles. Just as we have chiropractors who know our bodies and can adjust our backs into alignment, as well as nutritionists who advise us regarding diet and supplements, the safety of a multitude of counselors is sort of like a pit crew that has a designated amount of time to make sure our spiritual and emotional machine is in order before setting us back into the race. I believe the end-time warriors will actually get to this place spiritually. When the battle intensifies, and the excitement increases, the fighter knows the day he has prepared for is near. No fears. *No* regrets.

Now is the time when those who are pertinent to your destiny and promotion are surrounding you on all sides. You may have experienced loss of friends and family, but the ones who are with you now, I truly believe, will be the ones with you in the final days to come as well. These people, too, are end-game and game-changing warriors who carry similar experiences and fights within their bones, and the

Holy Spirit has most likely gathered them outside the four walls of your local church building.

As warriors, we will experience together whatever our opposition throws at us. We will experience a natural high because whether you win or lose, we are all there for this experience and your ultimate victory. It's like a professional fighter who is in his final cage fight! All the emotions now rush to the surface as your new warrior family cries, we get excited, want pictures, and we hug, encourage, and celebrate you! I have always said we will be celebrated not tolerated! No longer will the focus be on the popular preacher who takes the center ring for attention or the celebrity fighter who wants his name on the marquee. The focus will be on the gathering of everyone who was a part of your "training." There will be a team connection because we saw the game plan or the prophetic vision and we have all come together. This is the end-time army of believers! As Caleb declared, "Let us go up at once and possess it; *we* are well able to conquer it" (Numbers 13:30 AMPCE, italics mine). Warriors, we are living in the season of possession now! There's nothing we can't conquer when we come together with the mind-set of a fighter!

A CALL TO ACTION

- List those around you who are strong-minded and fueled by challenges and risk takers.
- What are some of the challenges you are currently facing that require risk?
- List "land(s)" God has promised but you have yet to acquire or win back.
- Do you have mature coaches or spiritual mentors who encourage you about when to rest and when to fight? In which season do you currently find yourself?

DAY 26

HOUSING HIS PRESENCE

Do you not know that your bodies are temples of the Holy Spirit, who is in you, whom you have received from God? You are not your own.

— 1 Corinthians 6:19

While I am fully aware many believers have heard this scripture over and over, I feel that we as Christ's body need to ask Him for a fresh revelation of what the verse really means. I sense deep within my bones, and I understand, the weightiness of housing His presence. My prayer is that within the pages of this devotional, I am able to articulate the seriousness of this scripture. Here's an undeniable fact: Our bodies don't belong to us. We are the property of the One who created us; and that should speak volumes in and of itself.

The first time I understood that our bodies are vessels to carry God's glory was when I witnessed my mother dying in hospice care. I had not seen her since I was nineteen years old (sadly, this was her decision). In 2009 I received a call from a cousin stating that the Holy Spirit had told her to call me. She faithfully prayed for my mother's and my relationship over the years and had heard that my mother was in hospice, moments from death. My cousin shared with me the heaviness the Holy Spirit had laid upon her heart. I knew my youngest daughter, Lauren, was to go with me. My heart began to race, knowing this would be the first time in twenty years I had seen my mother. I didn't know her condition, or if she even wanted to see me, but none of that mattered because I had chosen to be obedient during this pivotal moment in time. Plus, I had Lauren to consider, knowing she had never met her grandmother. How would she be received? My mother never accepted me, so I could only imagine the "warm welcome" my daughter might receive as well. Regardless, we boarded a plane as soon as we could, praying we would make it to the hospital in time to see my mother alive. God's timing was perfect, for we were at her bedside twenty-four hours before she took her final breath. I was briefed quickly by the doctors that the cause of her declining health was *emphysema*. The clinical term for emphysema is, "a disease in which the lungs become stretched and breathing becomes difficult"[1] (there is a spiritual correlation here).

As I entered the hospital room cautiously, I saw her helpless, frail body lying there, and I thought back to the last time I had seen my mother. I went for a brief visit in 1990 to introduce her to my soon-to-be husband. I recognized immediately the jealous and hateful spirit that defined her face and body language as we entered the house. As I was excitedly sharing our plans, all of a sudden, like a lunging animal, she placed both hands under the kitchen table and flipped it over! She began spewing venomous words to my fiancé. "Once you get to know her you will despise her," she snarled, "and you're old enough to be her father, so she'll leave you as soon as the money runs out."

If words could have been arrows, then an arsenal was shot at me. Each arrow had my name on it and was fashioned to take me out! As I think back on that day, I believe that was the first and only time my fiancé protected me. He grabbed my hand, and as we raced out of my childhood home, he told me he would never allow me to go back there again.

Sadly, my marriage to him would be a replay of my childhood. When we don't deal and heal from our past, we find familiar "comfort" in repeating it. I had never healed from this abuse and ended up marrying that same arsenal of arrows! That day, I left knowing I would never see my mother again; although, through the years, I respectfully sent cards and messages that went ignored.

I had grown up watching my mother smoke two packs of cigarettes a day. To accompany this addiction, she kept a pot of coffee going. When she wasn't drinking coffee, she poured glass after glass of Dr. Pepper. To this day I can visualize the two-liter bottles that lined the kitchen floor! Even at my young age, I knew enough to see she was killing herself slowly by the choices she was making. However, I also knew my father was cheating on her, and these habits were her way of tolerating life. Over the years I witnessed my gorgeous, healthy mother, who worked out in black leotards at Jack LaLanne health clubs, deteriorating on many levels. Her face no longer glowed with life and joy. She was filled with anger and depression and eventually traded her leotards for sloppy sweat suits. She filled her lonely hours with television soap operas, and that's exactly what she personified. Thanks to a steady diet of consuming drama and affairs on TV, gossip and hate overtook her life. She lived what she watched, and her temple housed all things impure! Through the years I prayed for reconciliation, but it never happened. Yet, on this day, God granted my prayer to see her! As I entered that room I could feel the demonic atmosphere. I approached her bed and began the process of asking forgiveness for pain I've caused as her daughter. Then I offered forgiveness for pain she had caused me. She was never conscious the entire time I was there, but I could tell her spirit recognized me. She growled and grimaced at my every word. It was obvious the sound of my voice made her angry. This is what nursing jealousy and unforgiveness will leave you with! Complete torment! I cried out to the Lord and asked Him why she couldn't awaken for one second to acknowledge me. My daughter looked at me and said rather matter-of-factly, "Mom, if she opens her eyes, she is going to punch you. Your mother hates you!" I asked Lauren to sing over my mother because she has an angelic singing voice. I understood in that very moment why Lauren was supposed to come.

Now, back to the root cause of emphysema! Spiritually speaking, the absence of air in our lungs is a physical manifestation of the very breath of God being squashed. Yes, smoking, marijuana use, air pollution, and chemicals all contribute to shortness of breath. But I know by the Spirit of God my mother's use of some of these pollutants was fueled by bitterness, anger, and unresolved issues in her life that stemmed from the incest she experienced at the hands her own father when she was sixteen years old! It is possible the day that this animal chose to rob her virginity he also stole the very air from her lungs. She literally lived with a minimized ability to take in oxygen! Most sexual abuse survivors, and especially rape victims, will tell you they couldn't breathe when they were being assaulted! Again, I am writing this book to bring to light how our physical conditions could possibly be linked to former, unresolved trauma. This isn't the case 100 percent of the time, but I can tell you that I've linked physical illnesses to emotional trauma with every client who has come to me for counseling or ministry! Yes, I said every single one! Now with pure abandon, I offer this wisdom and understanding on the pages of this book in the hope that even one person may be set free!

The presence of God abides in each of our temples, or bodies. We literally house the Holy Spirit. He is a person, and He lives within us to express the will of God and His Son, Jesus Christ. In truth, our temples are the "guest rooms" for the Holy Spirit to live and express the heart of Jesus on a daily basis, first to us, then to others. When I think of the magnificent miracle that God Himself would even desire to live within this human shell, my heart is filled with extreme gratitude but also responsibility. This temple absolutely is not my own. I am His property (in a healthy way). Have you ever heard the statement, "I am not your property?" or "I don't belong to you?" Even as I write this I am reminded of a story of a six-year-old child, who told her babysitter, "You're not the boss of me!" Yes, it's funny, although the parent didn't think so at the time; but, unlike a little child's bad attitude, we need to understand God *is* our boss and for our safety and well-being He expects us to obey His instructions. What an amazing honor to say we are His property.

Jesus is the King of kings and the Lord of lords. There is no other god beside him. Why would we fight against surrendering our bodies, and what we put in them, to Him? God can be trusted; He is not man that He should lie (Numbers 23:19).

If we do not belong to ourselves, then we must be very careful about what goes inside our bodies. Has it occurred to us that we are feeding God on a daily basis? After all, Jesus told the crowd that He and His Father are one (John 10:30). We shouldn't be surprised when our bodies reflect physically what we feed our mind and emotions. Power or pollution are the only two options available.

Just like my mother, myself, and countless others, someone or something in life may have attempted to take your breath away and leave behind the results of "spiritual emphysema," but what you choose to do with that trauma is up to you. Release those emotional and physical pollutants and replace them with the Word and nutrition! Let's treat our Guest with the utmost honor and respect. Our temples deserve five-star treatment! From here on out let's make conscious choices to care for our temples. It's your time to breathe once again!

A CALL TO ACTION

- Do you suffer from emphysema? If so, think back on an event that brought intense fear, panic, or breathlessness. If you don't suffer with this condition, do you still find yourself experiencing panic attacks or constriction of breath?

- As I indicated, my mother used addictions to escape reality. List the addictions you face currently.

- Meditate on one addiction (something you are either physiologically or psychologically bent toward).

- Pray and ask the Holy Spirit to show you what you're currently allowing into your temple that doesn't please Him.

DAY 27

IDENTIFYING END-TIME CARRIERS OF THE GLORY

Uzzah reached out and took hold of the ark of God . . . The LORD's anger burned against Uzzah because of his irreverent act; therefore God struck him down, and he died there beside the ark of God.

— 2 SAMUEL 6:6-7

Have you ever had the opportunity to take an all-inclusive vacation? Colorful advertisements entice us with gorgeous vacation spots from all around the world that cater to every kind of lifestyle. Whether you're single, married, or married with children, you can find fun-filled destinations that offer a variety of programs, fulfilling every desire possible. I thoroughly enjoyed all-inclusive vacations with my daughters, located throughout various regions of the Dominican Republic, Itapúa, and the beautiful Caribbean oceans. Each resort package always included airfare, food, drink, and exciting entertainment; however, not every location was alike. The locals have their own unique personalities, and the cuisines reflect the traditions of the land. At times foods were served that I didn't care for, or specific programs were offered that I had no interest in. Some resorts offered thrilling sporting events, while others focused more on the after-dinner entertainment for the children. I also recognized how hard each employee worked. It was easy to see the contrast between the lifestyles we are privileged to lead in comparison to the staff at the resorts. However, every worker poured their heart and soul into making all the visitors feel at peace and at home. I loved the convenience of calling for room service at all hours, especially in the morning. I looked forward to having my steaming cappuccino delivered bedside! An all-inclusive holiday releases us from having to worry about our needs and others for a brief while.

Today's scripture reading is centered on King David's becoming king over Israel. All the tribes of Israel came to David and spoke something extraordinary. "We are your own flesh and blood. In the past, while Saul was king over us, you were the one who led Israel on their military campaigns" (2 Samuel 5:1). This is dedication at its best; but even more, these men recognized the anointing upon their new king. All the leaders then made a treaty with David and anointed him king (verse 3). Imagine being handed this great responsibility at the young age of thirty! Soon thereafter, David chose thirty thousand men to bring the ark of God to Jerusalem. They placed it upon a new cart in order to transport it to Jerusalem. Uzzah and Ahio, Abinadab's sons, were guiding the cart (verses 1-4).

It's important to point out that Abinadab[1] was a Levite whose name means "My father is noble." He was the second of the eight sons of Jesse. We now see his sons driving this sacred cart while everyone was celebrating with all their might before the Lord with songs, harps, lyres, tambourines, and cymbals (verse 5). This must have been a sight to behold! All of a sudden, when they arrived at the threshing floor, one of the oxen stumbled, and Uzzah reached out and took hold of the ark. The Lord's anger blazed against Uzzah and struck him dead because of his irreverent act. David was so enraged because of God's deadly outburst against Uzzah that he called this place "Perez Uzzah" (verses 6-8), which means "breaking[2] of Uzzah or breakthrough." David started out super excited to carry the Glory with his military friends and lead all of Israel, but he quickly realized God is not going to accept man's way of religion. The men who transported the ark had good intentions, but they tried to do it a man's way! This had to be an "aha" moment for King David!

The perplexity of this story cannot be denied or ignored. God is speaking to us, and all of us had better heed his voice. Most certainly it would appear that Uzzah was attempting to do a good thing by steadying the ark. But we have to understand that what we think is good is not always God's way. In other words, just because we are doing what we deem to be good works, it doesn't mean these acts carry God's stamp of approval. Uzzah's good intentions turned out to have very deadly consequences in the sight of many! My sincerest concern is that the body of Christ understands the seriousness of carrying the glory of God, so that we, too, do not go the way of Uzzah. You may be quick to say that God's grace covers us; and if so, I present the question as to why this story is given to us in the Bible.

When I read that the whole house of Israel was singing, dancing, and celebrating, I picture worship services in many churches today. Everyone is excited as the worship team leads the congregation, but look at what happened in this passage after the celebration. They arrived at the threshing floor, which was used to separate grain. That is where Uzzah reached out and took hold of the ark of God.

Indeed, how wonderful it is to sing and dance before the Lord; however, leaders must be discerning that when His presence permeates the church, it's time to transition the people from celebration to dwelling in His glory! This must be done with reverence, care, and order! When the glory of God rests in our midst, no flesh can remain. In 1 Corinthians Paul tells us, "No flesh should glory in His presence" (1:29 NKJV). We serve a God of order, and He requires His people to worship Him "in spirit and truth" (John 4:24). The church cannot be about fun and games in the Spirit and leave out truth. I've been known to call this type of gathering the "dog and pony show," where leaders are about the gimmicks with no fear or concern for leading people into the glory of His presence. Only in His presence at the threshing floor will all our motives and ways be separated. The intents of our hearts aren't exposed in the dancing but in the dwelling of His presence.

I firmly believe the church is going to receive a serious wake-up call! My intention in saying that is not to be negative but rather informative. Just as all-inclusive vacations cater to our every need, I have witnessed an entitlement attitude permeating the church. We decide to visit a local church based upon researching all its "amenities," such as children's church, twelve-step recovery programs, choice of services times that are convenient to us, or the popularity of the preacher. We have become accustomed to our barista bar in the lobby; perhaps it serves a variety of our favorite coffees and creamers, and those who attend services fit into the mold of our own ideas of tradition. The entertainment is perfectly timed, the worship team does not sing too long, and holiday programs bring us comfort, peace, and a sense of familiarity. But what if you are needed at a specific location for someone else instead of being focused on your comfort? Just like the employees who serve others at the all-inclusive resorts, maybe what you have to offer will help other families who otherwise would never receive the privileges and spiritual freedoms you have experienced.

Just as King David had his "aha" moment, I believe many pastors will as well. They will understand that God desires that his glory be brought to His hurting people. He is searching for noble leaders who will allow Him in. The anointing breaks bondages; however, the manifested glory of God changes atmospheres.

It took David three months after Uzzah's death to figure out the proper procedure for transporting the glory. Once he followed God's procedure, the ark was brought safely to its place near the Holy City. The ark of God was so holy, God decreed that not even the Levites may touch or handle it. Only the priests could approach the ark. Where there is order and reverential fear, the glory of God will descend. If we learn anything from this story, it is that refusing to follow the directions or procedures God lays down can result in death: death of our destinies, dreams, visions, and, literally, premature physical death.

The church is not an all-inclusive getaway where the worship leaders run the program from the platform, nor should those who attend these services. We can't just "pick up the phone" at all hours of the night and place our orders with the pastors. These men and woman need order and reverential fear in the house if they want to become end-time carriers of the glory. Just as David named the place of Uzzah's death "Perez Uzzah," we, too, can expect a great "breaking" within our own houses before we will be called to step forward as God's chosen ones who are privileged to carry the glory.

A CALL TO ACTION

- Are you aware of the Holy Spirit's presence? If you answer no, ask Him to teach you how to be aware on a daily basis. If your answer is yes, ask the Him to reveal how you are to handle His presence.

- Are your actions or responses quick to do what you deem to be good or His will? Ask for wisdom to discern the difference.

- Are you in a local church because of what it offers or because it is where God has led you to attend? Be aware that attendance may be for a season. Don't have your name carved in the pew because God may choose to move you.
- Set aside quiet time just to worship. Write down a psalm and sing it to the Lord.

DAY 28

BATTLE OF MARATHON: SOMEONE HAS TO BE THE RUNNER

"Write the vision.
And make *it* plain on tablets,
That he may run who reads it."

— HABAKKUK 2:2 NKJV

The body of Christ, in my opinion, has come to the place of extreme fatigue and exhaustion. Various issues have contributed to this problem. When we reach our limits, everything is affected: from our own ability to be productive, to our job performance, and most importantly, our ability to give to our spouses and children. I would venture to say many of you reading this now are exhausted and spent! Have you heard the saying, "Insanity is doing the same thing over and over yet expecting a different result"?

Not everyone is a runner. That's apparent as my husband and I look out our window to see men and woman running through our neighborhood for exercise on a Saturday morning. It blesses my heart to watch them attempt to exercise, but it's obvious some have to work much harder than others. It's the ones who are straining to "go that extra mile" who burden my heart. I want to jump in alongside them and explain that there's a better way for them to achieve their desired results. I notice runners with a perfect stride, and they resemble a gazelle gliding down the block. However, the ones who must use every ounce of energy to put one foot in front of the other to even drag around the block will experience exhaustion quickly. For example, in the sport of basketball, the coach assigns positions for each athlete, but not everyone is passed the ball for a full-court press. An athlete with fast-twitch muscle fibers generates short bursts of strength but tires more quickly. Slow-twitch fibers recruit fuel slowly and can go for longer periods of time before they fatigue. The coach can identify this type of player as the best choice to take the ball down the court for the basket. It's important to understand your strengths as well as your limitations so you can effectively maximize your specific design.

I want to speak to you about a term known as *orderly recruitment*. Each of our muscles is divided into functional groups. In order for the body to accomplish successful movements, the motor units must join together in a systematic way to supply the force necessary to achieve strength. This is the way God designed our bodies. The smallest numbers of muscle fibers begin contracting first during a movement, followed by the motor units with the largest number of fibers, to allow for a smooth, strong muscle contraction. In addition a motor unit can be recruited to replace an already active motor unit that is experiencing great fatigue. In the simplest form of explanation, as long as calcium and ATP (energy) are available, the body will continue to pull on each other, and twitching of the muscles occurs. Many of these tiny "pulling events" cause another twitch. When many twitches occur in a row, this teamwork produces a larger force. As long as oxygen is present and is transported to the muscle cell, the ATP process continues. This is called *aerobic contraction*, meaning "using oxygen." Muscle fatigue occurs when the muscles experience a reduction in their ability to produce the force needed to accomplish the desired movement. Should it come as a surprise that motor units within a given muscle appear to be ranked? Units with higher rankings are recruited as force is needed to perform an action. The more units that are recruited, the greater force!

In the early 1990s, I attended the Upper Room Church in Westminster, California, under the leadership of Pastor Floyd Lawhon. This was during the early days of a wave of great revival meetings. Pastor Lawhon stood up one day to tell us he was being promoted to oversee the Assemblies of God Church, and he spoke of how perplexed he was. He went on to share that a great vision had been given to him for the Upper Room, yet he was leaving. An older woman, no more than five feet tall stood up while he was speaking. Pointing her arthritic finger toward the pulpit she said, "Brother Lawhon, just because God gave you the vision, doesn't mean you're the one to run with it."

To this day, those words of wisdom resound in my spirit. Pride wants to tell you that because you saw it, then you must also be the one to run with it. Remember orderly recruitment? We must recruit the "smaller muscle fibers" in order for the large muscle to move with great force and strength. When many short and fast twitches work together, a great force of strength is amassed! If the vessel is older and tired, then there will be a great loss of ATP energy.

As I stated above, not everyone is a runner! Some are called to preach the Word in their local churches, while others are called to travel from nation to nation with the sustained energy to keep moving. I've heard of revivalists from back in the day, who devoted themselves to a grueling travel schedule, all the while making doctor visits and increasing medications because they were exhausted. I once gave a word to a pastor when we attended a Baptist church. I warned him that he would experience turbulence if he went on a particular mission trip. I was called a false prophet and kicked out of the church because his plane never had turbulence! (You will recall in a previous devotion, I warned about sharing visions with people who will not understand the prophetic revelation). He did end up returning from that trip with a sickness that never left his body! Not all pastors who are called to care for their own city and flock should travel around the world unless God commissions them to do so.

Habakkuk 2:2 doesn't say to get the vision, write it, and then take off around the world. Let's read exactly what the verse says:

"Write the vision
And make *it* plain on tablets,
That he may run who reads it."

People who are filled with oxygen and ATP energy are the ones who can run marathons. This is the generation that is able to go the distance, yet leaders continue to do the same things, same conferences, and same tired methods over and over, expecting a fresh, new revival! But we are achieving the same old results and drawing the same old crowds. Where is the orderly recruitment of fresh fire, fresh oil, and fresh youth who are able to take your vision and run with it? The body of Christ is in an anaerobic state, meaning it has no oxygen. We need fresh wind warriors who are filled with ATP energy, breathing life into dry bones. These warriors will not replace the others but join forces. Remember, every single one of these muscle fibers, large and small, when joined together creates great force!

The Battle of Marathon was known as one of history's most famous military engagements. It took place in 490 BC, during the Persian invasion of Greece. Greece had only 192 casualties, while the Persians had 6,400. Legend has it there was a "runner" who ran to Athens with the news of great victory. Apparently, this run was more than 26 miles, and Pheidippides ran this distance to tell the good news.[1]

Currently, the body of Christ is experiencing too many casualties. The suicide, depression, and divorce rates alone are at their highest. Where are the modern-day runners in God's army? Who wants to volunteer to be the runner and take someone's great vision, even if it's not your own, all the way across the battlefield? During the Battle of Marathon, while warriors were on the front line fighting with spurts of great force and energy, the long-distance runner was needed to deliver the good news. I love this story, because if we incorporate not only spiritual gifting but physical conditioning of believers, then everyone will be placed in the perfect positions so the army of Christ will be victorious. I must say that all I witness is the highlighting of spiritual gifts, while the physical condition is ignored. A person can't even enter the armed forces without passing a physical! When someone is physically fit and healthy, jealousy arises in the camp. Maybe the person you are ignoring is the one God has called to carry your vision!

The body of Christ must begin to work strategically in bringing all our forces together. We need the involvement of slow- and fast-twitch muscle groups. We must call forth "orderly recruitment" so that all the body parts work efficiently and productively. We can avoid fatigue and overworked muscles that are giving out and causing injury to the rest the body. But unless we recognize our limitations, both spiritually and physically, we will fall out of formation. Fatigue, exhaustion, and premature death will continue. Orderly recruitment is the answer! Who knows if that one you recruit may be the very one capable of the twenty-six-mile run across battle lines to bring the good news, preventing millions of casualties. Calling all marathon runners!

A CALL TO ACTION

- List areas in which you feel exhausted or fatigued.

- Focus on one area per day, and be aware of possible outside factors that drain you.

- Write down and detail your vision. If you don't have one, ask God. He will show you.

- Pray about whose vision you can help make happen and/or how others can help you implement orderly recruitment.

DAY 29

RECOVERING THE AX-HEAD: CAN A PROPHET HELP YOU RECOVER WHAT HAS BEEN LOST?

The man of God asked, "Where did it sink?" When [the man] showed him the place, Elisha cut a stick and threw it there, and made the iron float. "Lift it out," he said. Then the man reached out his hand and took it.

— 2 Kings 6:6

Loss, unfortunately, is a natural part of life. No one is a stranger to the long-lasting, and sometimes permanent, effects that loss can have on our lives. Our minds remember each incident in detail; our wills either surrender to or fight against these traumas and our emotions react. Herein lies the mysteries to all of our behaviors as human beings. Every day we come in contact with people in our families, our workplaces, and on social media. We are expected to interact and communicate appropriately and maturely, but sometimes we find ourselves overreacting because we are "triggered" by certain people or situations. Notice that I used the pronoun *we* because we alone are responsible for our own actions and reactions. One thing is clear: we cannot change someone else; but we can change the way we respond to situations.

I learned this lesson very early on, and it's not always easy to look at ourselves when there's a conflict. Proverbs 15:1 tells us, "A gentle answer turns away wrath, / but a harsh word stirs up anger." We all have a tendency to point fingers at other people when their reactions are not what we would deem godly or appropriate. In any situation where conflict arises, even if we feel we are right, it's imperative that we examine our own actions. It's also important to note that if we avoid communication or avoid following-through with something we said or promised we would do, this, too, can stir up strife and anger.

When I was a young mother I enjoyed hanging out with a particular friend. Whenever we would make plans to meet somewhere this person was consistently late. Her punctuality issues irritated me, mostly when the two of us had plans to see a movie. Inevitably I would be the first one to arrive at the theater. With each passing minute I would become more and more agitated, as I paced back and forth outside the theater and checked my watch every five minutes until it was time for the movie to start. Finally I would spot my friend running through the parking lot. It didn't seem to bother her that she was late. I missed the start of more good movies! Then on one of these occasions I heard the Lord speak to my heart, "Why do you continue to expect your friend to be on time when you know she's not capable of being punctual? The next time you make plans to go see a movie tell her you will meet her inside and you'll save her a seat." There was the answer! Thank you, Lord! The problem was solved, and my friend could be as late as she wanted or needed to be! But, other than the obvious reasons why people do not enjoy waiting around for their tardy friends, there was something deeper inside of me that "triggered" my intense reaction.

During my childhood my father expected certain things of me, of course, but he would also ask me to do things for him at the most inopportune times—times that suited him. My father particularly enjoyed back rubs. Sometimes when he asked for a back rub I would comply and rub his back; but on the evenings when he could see I was exhausted from a full day of school and sports practice, he still wanted me to rub his back, and I would politely tell him no. My father's passive-aggressive response was to use my refusal against me; so, the next time I needed something he would smugly say no. I tucked all these little episodes away in my mind, and as the years progressed I felt I had to be the one to make sure everyone had their needs met. I also realized that I had formed my opinion of my heavenly Father according to the conditional love of my earthly father. I developed a "If I scratch God's back, He will scratch mine" mentality. Could my father's response to me as a child be considered a loss? Absolutely! I grew up without the unconditional love of a father, which shaped my opinion of myself, how I responded to others, and, ultimately, my God.

After I received the revelation concerning my friend's lack of punctuality, the course of healing my soul was set. I had been turning my own inner hurt and disappointment toward my friend, expecting her to give me something she was not capable of giving. My mind recalled the childhood events with my father, and I fought against anyone who even remotely disrespected me in the same way.

Let's set the scene for our devotional reading. In 2 Kings 6 we read that a company of prophets lived with Elisha the prophet. One day these prophets approached Elisha and said, "You can see that this place where we're living under your leadership is getting cramped—we have no elbow room. Give us permission to go down to the Jordan where each of us will get a log. We'll build a roomier place" (verses 1-2 MSG). So Elisha granted them permission. The prophets asked Elisha to accompany them, and he did. Elisha's decision to go was a good one because as one of the men was cutting down a tree his ax-head came loose and flew into the water. "Oh no, master . . . it was borrowed!" (verses 2-5 MSG). You can sense the panic.

The first point I want to make is that all the prophets were hanging out together. It became obvious they needed more space, so out of respect for Elisha who was leading the group, they asked for permission to build out. Elisha said, "Go ahead." There's a saying among prophets, and it goes like this: "I know all about you; can you tell me what's going on with me?" There's no doubt in my mind why the prophets asked Elisha to join them; they understood each other.

First Corinthians 14 says, "The spirits of the prophets are subject to the prophets" (verse 32 NKJV). We prophets think alike and understand each other. We also understand we "know in part and we prophesy in part" (1 Corinthians 13:9), so there's safety when we expand and grow together. So, in our story, we read that as one of these prophets was cutting down a tree the head of his ax flew off into the Jordan River. He panicked that he had borrowed this ax from someone, which indicates to me that he didn't own his own ax. In a frenzy, he called out to his leader to help locate it. Elisha asked him an important question: "Where did it fall?" (verse 6). This leader knew how to deal with the emotional response of the one whom he was leading. When the man pointed to the spot, Elisha picked up a branch and threw it in the river. The iron ax-head floated to the top of the water.

Poverty and lack are interesting spirits that work side by side. While these spirits are not from the Lord, He allows us seasons of dealing with both so we have the opportunity to get to the root of issues from our past. When the prophet exclaimed, "It was borrowed!" we ask why panic was his initial response. He could've cried, "There goes my ax. This build-out is going to take a little longer that we had planned." Or maybe he could've responded, "I don't want to dive in and try to find this by myself. Who else is game?" Elisha understood the root of his response and threw a branch in the very spot it had been lost! A branch is an extension of a trunk (the main part of an artery or nerve). No doubt losing this ax-head struck a nerve in this poor guy, and his response was sheer panic! He knew if he couldn't dive down and recover it he would have to buy his friend a brand new one. Because these prophets understood they must stay together, the very presence of their leader gave them protection and revelation. When Elisha saw the head rise to the surface, he told the prophet to lift it up out of the water (verse 7).

Ephesians 4:11-13 tells us, "Christ himself gave the apostles, the prophets, the evangelists, the pastors and teachers, to equip his people for works of service, so that the body of Christ may be built up until we all reach unity in the faith and in the knowledge of the Son of God and become mature, attaining to the whole measure of the fullness of Christ." Because the prophets in the Elisha story understood order and authority, they continued to build out their dwelling, and they also received inner healing and encouragement as they worked together.

I want to point out the meaning of an ax-head. The ax-head is the cutting portion of a heavy blade. It is mounted on a handle and can be pushed between two things to separate them. Have you ever felt as if you were an ax-head in the hand of God? In your faithfulness to God, you have been the ax, or tool, cutting and separating what God wanted removed, and now you find yourself in a panic wondering how you will ever pay for what was lost. Let me encourage you, that the price has already been paid! You owe nothing.

I prophesy into your spirit that the time has come to locate and retrieve everything you have lost! The Lord will reveal to you the exact place you lost something dear to you and were traumatized. Your ax-head may have been separated from its handle, but you're about to *get a handle* on things you thought could never be recovered! Once you receive the revelation to locate that which has fallen into the deep, you only have to reach out your hand and reclaim it. Reach out, reclaim, and rejoice!

A CALL TO ACTION

- Write down a significant loss that may have come to mind while you were reading.
- List the emotions that are tied to that loss.
- Pray and ask God how to go about recovering what you have lost. If you're dealing with the loss of a loved one, ask God to show you specific, constructive ways to deal with your grief.
- Think about the expectations you place on others. Are they realistic? Are they tied to expectations your parents placed on you?

DAY 30

PULLING THE TRIGGER: IT'S A SETUP!

God didn't *set us up* for an angry rejection but for salvation by our Master, Jesus Christ. He did for us, a death that *triggered* life.

— 1 THESSALONIANS 5:9-10 MSG, ITALICS MINE

Counselors use the term *triggers* when working with our clients who come to us for answers concerning an ongoing problem. The term refers to something that "sets off" a memory tape or a flashback and transports a person back to the event of his or her original trauma. Generally, by the time people schedule an appointment, their ability to control their emotions has hit rock bottom. Some have found "safety" in completely withdrawing from the *source* that triggers their emotions. As I have shared previously, some warriors tend to fight off their enemy by withdrawing. However, once these warriors hit the threshold of pure exhaustion, the enemy begins to pick them off day by day and thought by thought. In order to survive they unknowingly end up with an addiction in the hopes of maintaining a state of pseudo euphoria, or a false sense of well-being. Sadly, many warriors are lost to suicide or overdose.

Warriors all around the world suffer alone and have become very skilled at remaining undercover. I am speaking of warriors who have fought courageously for our freedoms in the military as well as believers who have fought for the gospel of truth only to be targeted by religious snipers. When someone begins to retreat from his or her original trauma, the downward spiral will eventually become inevitable. These warriors are ticking time bombs. At some point, the resulting anger will become so explosive that it becomes impossible for him or her to respond with any wisdom or self-control. For a time, they've been able to keep their addiction to pornography, adultery, drinking, or gambling under control; but, eventually, the house of cards will collapse. As a counselor, I state how important it is for friends and family members of these warriors to be *empathetic* (the ability to identify with and understand somebody else's feelings or difficulties) and *compassionate*, to a degree, because the bottom line is, the anger is a result of unresolved hurt. I believe many of them are blaming God for their inability to be freed from their anger because pastors and leaders (and now social media "mentors") have made attempts to counsel but without godly insight into the soul.

A distinct difference exists in discerning between the spirit, soul, and body. When an inner conflict occurs between the different components that make up a person's individuality, he or she cannot function to his or her full potential as child of God. The spirit must rule and govern, but the soul must be healed! The soul is where the mind, will, and emotions reside, and many people are ruled by their soul and not their spirit.

Picture a circle in your mind. Located within that circle is every hurt, betrayal, adversity, and traumatic experience in your life. When seeking deliverance from trauma it's imperative to be under the care of someone who is ruled by the spirit but also understands the complexities of the soul. There are various styles of counseling, including confrontation, directive, encouragement, and exhortation. It's important to use wisdom when speaking with someone because you cannot approach every person using the same style. People are unique and special and must be handled with care and wisdom.

Over and over again, I have witnessed leaders' attempts to

counsel by decreeing and declaring only Scripture over people without implementing balanced care. My God! People are leaving their counseling sessions in worse mental and spiritual condition than when they walked in and blaming God because nothing changed!

As I have prophesied previously, all three "houses" are being cleaned up. The heart of the Father has been wrenched for the suffering of His people. As we witness the world in total chaos, we must understand God isn't surprised and indeed a "controlled chaos" exists. I know that term seems to be an oxymoron, but it's true.

When Donald Trump was running for president, I began to see God's plan unfolding in a new way. I started hearing comments from female Christian leaders. I noticed one of two responses when one by one this man's infidelities began to surface. Either they spoke out against him from their pulpits, convinced that Mr. Trump couldn't be God's "Cyrus-anointed" because he was an egotistical adulterer, or they remained silent and chose not to publicly stand up for him.

Let me say this: As a strong, outspoken female preacher myself, who has been healed from being sexually molested, date-raped, and addicted, as well as having been brutalized by male pastors and leaders in the church, I recognized exactly what was happening. When a person, whether male or female, has been through trauma, he or she will refer that pain to another source. Clinically speaking, this is called "referred pain."[1] When the body feels distress, suffering, or agony, the nerve endings are stimulated. The purpose for referred pain is to protect tissue from further damage, so it removes or withdraws from the source. When a man feels *overpowered,* instead of *empowered* by a woman, you will notice he is the one who raises his voice in the church expressing that it's unbiblical for a woman to lead. You may notice some who have been "triggered" in meetings, as male voices rise up against the women. I will also venture to say that some of these men are secretly viewing pornography, which causes not a love for women but disdain. This brings me back to what I noticed with the female preachers against President Trump. Each one of them has a background of abuse with men. If you look into their testimonies, my point will be substantiated. However, it's not my intention to call them out. We are all in need of healing, but God is making specific areas known so we can be made whole. Those of us who understand that God appointed this president certainly don't excuse his behavior but support him publicly while praying for the refinement of his soul. Because we've experienced complete healing in the abused areas of our souls, we recognize God's plan. This is why you may recognize some leaders that are right-on when they teach on a particular subject but completely miss truth in another. We are imperfect beings for sure; but if we do not seek healing for unresolved trauma, we will suck others into our emotional war zones, acting as magnets for people who have been damaged in the same ways. On the other hand, we will usher others into emotional and spiritual freedom!

We all know God uses other people to refine us. Men and women are brought into our lives to sharpen that which is dull and heal that which is hurting. Even Jesus declared in Luke 12:51, "Do you think I came to bring peace on earth? No, I tell you, but division." If we are not careful, we will always think God is refining someone else instead of ourselves! How we react to the lawlessness and evil in our nation and in our churches will reveal impurities within our own hearts and "trigger" unresolved issues.

Everywhere I go the "Red Sea" parts; people either receive me or they don't. I have yet to experience middle ground. How I react to their responses shows whether or not I need to allow the Holy Spirit further into the circle of hurt that surrounds my soul and receive healing. The most amazing truth about today's scripture reading is this: His death triggered life. I would like to encourage everyone who has read through, meditated, and prayed over these devotional readings to know that every area where you have experienced death has only been a setup to trigger life. As believers, when we understand that death is the beginning of life, this knowledge should encourage all of us to examine closely those areas that are triggering pain. When we choose to take a good hard look into our souls, true life can come forth. Yes, raw truth will feel as if someone is pulling the trigger and shooting more bullets toward whatever caused your trauma. Always remember, though, Jesus allowed your trial so that new life in that area can ultimately spring forth. Only the dead can be raised—not the living—and we all know what happened when Jesus died and rose again! What appeared as a *setback* on the cross was really the Father's *setup* for the gift of life to be given to all who would receive it.

Many of you who are reading this book may already be saved; meaning, you have given your spirit over to Jesus as your Lord and Savior. Now, He is asking you to trust Him by surrendering your mind, will, and emotions. God didn't set you up for a life of anger and rejection but for the saving of your own soul and the souls of others who will be inspired and encouraged by your victorious example! A setback? No! A setup!

A CALL TO ACTION

- Make a list of things that set you off (people, situations, places).
- Identify your reactions to these triggers and make a list.
- When conflict arises do you tend to think God is refining someone other than you?
- Name someone in your life who is being used to sharpen you. Be aware that it may be someone you avoid.

AFTERWORD

BY BRIAN "MR. UNBREAKABLE" WARREN

ON A RECENT TRIP to see my little girl in California, the Holy Spirit began speaking to me about my wife, Gina Guy-Warren, and the mantle on her life. One night we stopped at a coffee shop to relax. Anytime I enter into a public place, I scan the room, and this night was no different. I spotted a well-dressed, older man wearing a trench coat. A woman was paying for her coffee when "creepy man" lifted his hand slowly to touch her. I told Gina immediately that something didn't seem right as I directed her attention towards what I saw. It was obvious this woman didn't know him. Without pause Gina became agitated and made her way over to let the woman know what was going on. At that moment it was clear to me the extent of my wife's gifting, as if I didn't already know! When I first met Gina in 2013, I was an "armor bearer" for her ministry (guard and protect as she ministers); and I witnessed things I had never seen before as a Christian—supernatural moves of God as well as some people that I call "fake Christians" who hovered in and around her ministry. Before we were even dating, I had a vision of Gina standing on a platform with a sea of people in front of her, similar to when you see preachers on huge platforms in Africa where thousands go down in the Holy Spirit as they open their mouths. I knew millions of people would be saved at the sound of her voice!

After we were married, I had a second vision. We were on our way to a funeral in California for a true, authentic prophet for whom I had great respect, when I glanced over at my wife. I was caught up in a vision I will never forget. Gina looked exactly like him! I realized they had the same spirit. At the time that was only the third vision God had given me. That day opened my eyes even more to this woman's heart and purpose.

My wife is a person of action, and that is why many people shy away from her. I have the privilege of witnessing the countless dreams and visions she receives on a daily basis. The various ways God speaks to her are really awesome to watch. She will read people and "their mail," so to speak; that's not good, if you're all jacked up and trying to hide something. There is neither procrastination nor hesitation in Gina. She exhibits immediate obedience. That's why this book is so important for such a time as this! All believers as well as non-believers seriously need to read it.

I was reading my Bible on a flight shortly after receiving this revelation, and the light bulb turned on. In John 18 we read about the arrest of Jesus but verse 37 caught my attention: "You are a king, then!" said Pilate. Jesus answered, "You say that I am a king. In fact, the reason I was born and came into the world is to testify to the truth. *Everyone on the side of truth listens to me*" (italics mine).

There it is, folks! Jesus knew both His call and purpose on this earth, and so does my wife, Gina! The *truth-tellers* in this world and the *truth-seekers* will love this type of revelatory teaching. The fakes and lukewarm people will be exposed. I coined the phrase "fake Christians" before President Trump called out the "fake news." You can run but you can't hide. The fire has now been turned up. Little white lies and any and all sin will be brought to the surface. God isn't playing around! He is coming for a spotless bride, not a messed up one. Mark my words. My wife has been prophesying since 2015 that God is cleaning all three houses! The White House, Courthouse, and the church house. Time is short; and ready or not, He is now coming to your house.

Gina has always said there's a difference between the wicked and the weak. For those who are doing right, He will sharpen you up to be better Christians. The sharpening might sting a little, but it's for your benefit. But to all who are wicked and carry out evil motives: if you don't repent and change your ways, God will use you as a public example, and it will be to your demise.

Gina Guy-Warren was born to expose truth, whether good, bad, or indifferent. What others might let slip by or slide through the cracks, Gina will not. She is priceless and would lay her life down for a complete stranger. I am so proud of this woman!

No one but the Lord and me sees what Gina has overcome and currently fights through spiritually and physically. I don't know anyone else like her. I'm thankful God gave this woman to me as my wife. She has helped clean me up from a lingering sin. I know she is the real deal because I have sat through and slept through countless sermons and Bible studies before I met her. The sin I dealt with never broke from me until I met her. I am forever grateful, and I know there are other men and women who need her because, like me, they can't break free on their own. They may claim to be wise with tons of spiritual experience, but they don't have the "breaker-anointing" that Gina carries. She might be a little intense, but can you blame her? Look how messed up this world is, and even worse, the church! People are dying and committing suicide on our watch, and that's not OK! Who will step up and join forces with us? I hear only empty talk that results in no action. Instead of hearing the sound of war drums, I hear the sound of crickets in the night— "fake Christians" full of talk and lengthy prayers but no action. It might be safe to say a high percentage of the people on this earth are either on prescription or illegal drugs. Maybe they are self-medicating to forget their pain, even over drinking alcohol in order to forget what's truly hurting them. Rather than going after their healing, they continue to open more windows to many of Satan's clever and evil traps. Gina will find and expose the root to the entry points of pain and trauma in one's life.

The job of a prophet is definitely not a popular one. Millions of people will follow those who give a *candy-coated, one-size-fits-all prophecy that speaks of great things to come.* We all recognize preachers who are "nice and fluffy, easy does it, don't rock the boat, I made it to the Prophets and Seer's list with my prophetic word-of-the-month message." Gina's calling is to help God's people become set free completely. I believe she is the best at what she does and has the purest heart I've ever seen.

Speaking from experience, I've witnessed hundreds of real breakthroughs and testimonies. Gina may not make the earthly social media lists or travel within the popular prophetic social cliques, but her words are most assuredly written upon the scrolls of heaven. I know my wife, and that's all that matters to her. An audience of one!

Sadly I've seen many people, especially Christian leaders, manipulate with hidden agendas. Their motives are to get something for themselves and use God's wounded for selfish gain. Many of these leaders pretend they don't notice Gina or recognize her gifting. I see their jealousy and fear brought on by their own insecurities. If they were to join forces with Gina, then somehow, they might lose their own following and the tithe money that comes along with it! Even in the past, there were some who partnered with her, then took their money and ran when truth came too close for comfort. Gina still loves, forgives, and presses through. That's my wife; all in for Jesus and righteousness, no matter the cost!

Look at what President Trump is doing in the White House. He's cleaning it out with his words, tweets, and actions. I believe my wife has been called to the body of Christ to clean it up with her words and actions. I call her "Baby Trumpet." Like it or not, I'll be standing right next to her as she executes her God-given mantle. She never has to recruit disciples but always leads simply by example. Gina is a rare commodity these days because her heart is so pure. As I am writing I am motivated to be more like her in the area of ministry.

Search her video messages on our YouTube channel, "Truth-N-

Love Ministry International, The WARrens." I believe she's a prototype for this generation of how to walk the walk and how to act and treat one another. Gina is a rare gift to the body of Christ, and I'm honored to share her with the world!

"The Husband"

APPENDIX A: ZIJA INTERNATIONAL® WELLNESS SUPPLEMENTS

Moringa Oleifera

Moringa oleifera is harvested in India where the richest soil in the world can be found. Zija™ brand *Moringa oleifera* is the only enzymatically alive Moringa on the planet, which means the body will absorb 100 percent within minutes.

Testimonial

In thirty-five years in the health and wellness industry, we have never seen a product do so much for so many. It is my honor to partner with Truth-N-Love Ministry International/The Word and the Workout. I've known Pastor Brian Warren for many years, and now his wife Pastor Gina Guy-Warren for the past four years. Their hearts are to see every life with whom they come in contact change.

Respectfully,
Rory and Carmilla Wendell , Owners, Fitness World Health Club, Former competitive bodybuilder, Semi-Pro football player, Zija International® Emerald

Supermix™ and SmartMix™

Do you or someone you know suffer from arthritis, diabetes, depression, anxiety, high blood pressure, lupus, fibromyalgia, eczema, Parkinson's, cancer, or obesity? This amazing product contains ninety-two nutrients, thirty-six anti-inflammatories, all essential amino acids, and more!

I recommend that you start with Supermix/Premium Detox Tea.[1, 2] Supermix is organic, kosher, gluten-free, and a Halal-certified whole food providing 400 to 600 percent of the daily vitamin and mineral requirements. This supplement *replaces* your current multivitamin and fish oil/fatty acid supplements and can act as a meal replacement. Supermix is *not* a super juice; it is a food. (If you take various medications, begin with SmartMix, since the delivery of nutrient is slower to the system.)

XMpm™

Do you have trouble sleeping? Check out Zija's XMpm.

Zija International® products carry a 100 percent money-back guarantee. To order Zija products please visit www.PastorGina.MyZija.com or www.MrUnbreakable.MyZija.com. Free consultation when ordering any Zija products is available at (951) 833-8190.

We are also in the PDR (Physician's Desk Reference). Zija Moringa Supermix, plant protein, and other products are now officially prescribed by doctors!

APPENDIX B: COUNSELING SERVICES

Gina Guy-Warren is available for counseling. If you do not reside in the Franklin, Tennessee area, counseling is available via Skype. (A donation of $100 or $50 for Team Unbreakable financial partners is requested.)

Truth-N-Love Ministry International
1113 Murfreesboro Rd, Suite 106-222
Franklin, Tennessee
Office: (951) 833-8190
www.TNLMI.org / www.TheWordandTheWorkout.org

NOTES

Day 1

1. E. Scott Reckard, "Barry Minkow Gets 5 Years For Embezzling from San Diego Church," *L.A. Times*, April 28, 2014, https://www.latimes.com/business/la-fi-minkow-sentence-20140429-story.html.
2. Roger Parloff, "Barry Minkow: All-American Con Man," *Fortune* magazine, January 5, 2012, http://fortune.com/2012/01/05/barry-minkow-all-american-con-man/.
3. Parloff, "Barry Minkow: All-American Con Man."

Day 2

1. Dictionary.com, s.v. "incubate (*v., used with object*)," accessed March 21, 2019, https://www.dictionary.com/browse/incubate.

Day 3

1. Rebecca Joseph, "Trump clears medical test: Doctor administered Montreal Cognitive Assessment," last updated January 16, 2018, https://globalnews.ca/news/3968959/trumps-medical-test-montreal-cognitive-assessment/.

Day 4

1. *Merriam-Webster's Collegiate Dictionary*, 11th ed., s.v. "kindle," (Springfield, MA: Merriam-Webster, 2003). Continually updated at https://www.merriam-webster.com/.

Day 5

1. "Lion Attacked by Pack of Hyenas," Dynasties, BBC Earth, YouTube video, November 26, 2018, https://www.youtube.com/watch?v=a5V6gdu5ih8.

Day 6

1. *Merriam-Webster's Collegiate Dictionary*, 11th ed., s.v. "combat."
2. "Five Things Monsanto Doesn't Want You to Know about GMOs," Food and Water Watch, May 7, 2015, https://www.foodandwaterwatch.org/print/news/five-things-monsanto-doesnt-want-you-know-about-gmos.
3. "Gene Gun Method," *Maximum Yield* magazine, accessed March 25, 2019, https://www.maximumyield.com/definition/3145/gene-gun-method.
4. "Gene Gun Method," Maximum Yield magazine.
5. Leslie Carol Botha, "Are gender-bending chemicals causing gender confusion?" The Liberty Beacon, accessed March 25, 2019 http://www.thelibertybeacon.com

Day 8

1. *Merriam-Webster's Collegiate Dictionary*, 11th ed., s.v. "atrophy."

Day 9

1. World Without Genocide, "Rwandan Genocide," accessed March 27, 2019, http://worldwithoutgenocide.org/genocides-and-conflicts/rwandan-genocide.

Day 10

1. *Merriam-Webster's Collegiate Dictionary*, 11th ed., s.v. "sedative."

Day 11

1. Abarim-publications.com.,"Etymology of the name Josheb-Basshebeth," http://www.abarim-publications.com/Meaning/Josheb-basshebeth.html#.XMjbs5NKicY.
2. Abarim-publications.com.,"Etymology of the name Josheb-Basshebeth," http://www.abarim-publications.com/Meaning/Josheb-basshebeth.html#.XMjbs5NKicY.
3. *Merriam-Webster's Collegiate Dictionary*, 11th ed., s.v. "vice."
4. Abarim-publications.com, "Etymology of the name Eleazar," http://www.abarim-publications.com/Meaning/Eleazar.html#.XMjcTJNKicY.
5. Abarim-publications.com, "Etymology of the name Shammah," http://www.abarim-publications.com/Meaning/Shammah.html#.XMjcfZNKicY.

Day 14

1. *Merriam-Webster's Collegiate Dictionary*, 11th ed., s.v. "presuppose."
2. *Merriam-Webster's Collegiate Dictionary*, 11th ed., s.v. "lukewarm."

Day 17

1. "Roe v. Wade, 410 U.S. 113 (1073)," Opinions, Justia, US Supreme Court, accessed April 1, 2019, https://supreme.justia.com/cases/federal/us/410/113/.
2. "AT HOME WITH: Norma McCorvey; Of Roe, Dreams And Choices," The New York Times, July 28, 1994, https://www.nytimes.com/1994/07/28/garden/at-home-with-norma-mccorvey-of-roe-dreams-and-choices.html.
3. "Brief History of the Abortion Pill in the U.S.," *Web*MD Health News, September 28, 2000, https://www.webmd.com/women/news/20000928/brief-history-of-abortion-pill-in-us#1.
4. "Israel Celebrates 70 Years of Independence," Israel Ministry of Foreign Af-fairs, April 18, 2018, https://mfa.gov.il/MFA/AboutIsrael/Spotlight/Pages/Israel-celebrates-70-years-of-independence-18-April-2018.aspx.
5. "Age at Inauguration," POTUS, Presidents of the United States, accessed April 1, 2019, https://www.potus.com/presidential-facts/age-at-inauguration/.

Day 18

1. *Merriam-Webster's Collegiate Dictionary*, 11th ed., s.v. "infiltrates."

Day 19

1. "Who Is Affected by Bipolar Disorder?" Bipolar Disorder Statistics, Depression and Bipolar Support Alliance, accessed April 2, 2019, https://www.dbsalliance.org/education/bipolar-disorder/bipolar-disorder-statistics/.
2. Aurelie Corinthios, "Charlie Sheen Concedes He 'Might' Be Bipolar: 'I've Come This Far, Might as Well Fix It All,'" accessed April 14, 2019 www.people.com/tv/charlie-sheen-says-he-might-be-bipolar-on-dr-oz/.
3. Christina Heiser, "Demi Lovato Speaks Up About Living With Bipolar Disorder" www.womenshealthmag.com/health/a19925262/demi-lovato-be-vocal-campaign.
4. Dory Jackson, "Kate Spade Might Have Had Bipolar Disorder and Refused Treatment, Sister Says. June 6, 2018, www.newsweek.com/kate-spade-sistr-reveals-bipolar-disorder-962178.
5. Underpress.net, "Robin Williams and Manic Depression: Bipolar Disorder Doesn't Choose," accessed April 15, 2019, http://undepress.net/robin-williams-and-manic-depression-bipolar-disorder-doesnt-choose/.
6. Leslie Messer, "Demi Lavato: How I Treat My Bipolar Disorder," May 1, 2014

https://abcnews.go.com/Entertainment/demi-lovato-treat-bipolar-disorder/story?id=23538615

7. James Strong, Strong's Exhaustive Concordance of the Bible, "pharmakeia: the use of medicine, drugs or spells Strongs Concordance 5331 Greek https://biblehub.com/greek/5331.htm.
8. Spiros Zodhiates-John Kohlenberger, The Hebrew-greek Key Study Bible: New International Version, s.v. "Ruah" #8120 (AMG, International Inc., 1996).

Day 20

1. "When you don't feel at home about your gender," September 23, 2018, https://www.webmd.com/sex/gender-dysphoria#1.

Day 24

1. National Resource Center on ADHD, "About ADHD Fact Sheet," CHADD, accessed April 3, 2019, https://chadd.org/wp-content/uploads/2018/03/aboutADHD.pdf.
2. Stacy Simon, "What's Wrong with Hot Dogs, Hamburgers, and Bacon?" American Cancer Society, June 25, 2018, https://www.cancer.org/latest-news/hot-dogs-hamburgers-bacon.html.

Day 26

1. *Merriam-Webster's Collegiate Dictionary*, 11th ed., s.v. "emphysema."

Day 27

1. Abarim-publications.com, "Etymology of the name Abinadab," http://www.abarim-publications.com/Meaning/Abinadab.html#.XMSSLmhKiUk.
2. Abarim-publications.com, "Etymology of the name Perez Uzzah" http://www.abarim-publications.com/Meaning/Perez-uzzah.html#.XMjatpNKicY.

Day 28

1. "Battle of Marathon," Greek History, Encyclopaedia Brittanica, accessed April 4, 2019, https://www.britannica.com/event/Battle-of-Marathon.

Day 30

1. The Free Dictionary.com, s.v. "Referred Pain," Medical Dictionary, http://medical-dicionary.thefreedictionary.com/referred+pain.

Appendix A: Zija International® Wellness Supplements

1. Supermix and our Vegan Plant Protein are listed in the PDR (*Physicians' Desk Reference*).
2. Mayo Clinic uses our Améo™ essential oils.

ABOUT THE AUTHOR

Gina Guy-Warren has served in full-time ministry for more than twenty-five years and is the founder of Truth-N-Love Ministry International. She and her husband, Brian Warren, MMA Fight Champion, defend, mobilize, train, and equip those who have been hurt by life and religion. Gina is a confidant to many leaders who suffer in private and is a revivalist teaching how to move in the Holy Spirit. She founded The Word and the Workout, which is a unique fitness ministry that combines physical fitness with focused discipline, and she has also trained Homeland Security personnel. Gina has traveled throughout many countries in Africa, including South Sudan as Vice-president of International Relief, founding a school in the Congo. She was instrumental in the healing of the Congolese people after the genocide between Rwanda/Congo, all while working medical clinics. She implemented entrepreneur workshops for the widows and teachers. Gina is the mother of two daughters and Brian's daughter. Gina and Brian currently reside in Franklin, Tennessee

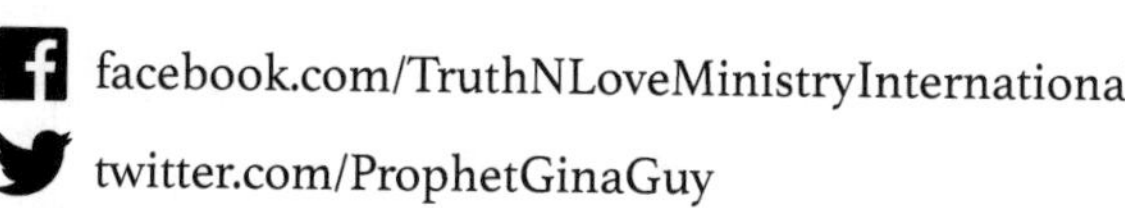

facebook.com/TruthNLoveMinistryInternational
twitter.com/ProphetGinaGuy
instagram.com/wordandtheworkout

ALSO BY THE WARRENS

Unbreakable Love is the story of one mans unbreakable love for his daughter, and about God's unbreakable love for him, despite his faults and failings as a man. Known as Mr.Unbreakable in the ring and cage, Brian Warren has delivered by Earning 2 title Belts and battling some of the best fighters in the world, including UFC fighters Cung Le, Karo Parisyan, and Ben Saunders. And though Brian hasn't always won—in life or the ring—his spirit remains unbreakable. This is a story of courage, unwavering devotion, and determination to rise from the ashes and to stand once again as a champion, and this time for the glory of God and his beloved daughter, Breesa. Brian's story will inspire you to be a better man, father, and disciple, and to never give up on yourself and certainly not on your dreams.

Available on Amazon. Pick up a copy today.